# CONTENTS

**ALEXANDRA DAVID-NEEL** was born in Paris in 1868, the only child of Louis Pierre David, who fled to exile with his friend Victor Hugo after Louis Napoleon's rightist coup in 1851. Hugo's celebrated daughter Adèle pursued a young army officer to America and went mad with grief. David's daughter became one of the world's great adventurers. At 18, Alexandra walked across the Alps to Italy. In the 1880s she rode a bicycle from Brussels to Spain. In her early twenties, she made her first journey East, through Ceylon and India, until her money ran out and she was forced to return to France and support herself as an opera singer. At the age of 35 she was married. Five days after the wedding, the marriage dissolved. In 1912, the Dalai Lama granted David-Neel the first private interview ever given to a Western woman. From then on she plunged deeper into Tibetan mysticism, trekking across snow-covered mountains for weeks at a time to reach isolated temples and teachers. Finally, in 1924, she penetrated Lhasa, the Forbidden City of Tibet, and witnessed the strange rituals of Lamaism. Her more than 20 books, including MY JOURNEY TO LHASA, THE SUPERHUMAN LIFE OF GESAR OF LING, MAGIC AND MYSTERY IN TIBET, and THE SECRET ORAL TEACHINGS IN TIBETAN BUDDHIST SECTS, provide one of the best records of a culture now threatened by extinction. She ended her days in a Tibetan-style house she built in the Basses-Alps. She died in 1969, at the age of 100.

# BUDDHISM

## ITS DOCTRINES AND ITS METHODS

## ALEXANDRA DAVID-NEEL

## with a foreword by
## Christmas Humphreys

A DISCUS BOOK/PUBLISHED BY AVON BOOKS

This is a reprint of the authorized English translation by
H.N.M. Hardy and Bernard Miall of the French volume:
LE BOUDDHISME, SES DOCTRINES ET SES
METHODES


AVON BOOKS
A division of
The Hearst Corporation
959 Eighth Avenue
New York, New York 10019

Foreword Copyright © 1977 by The Bodley Head
Published by arrangement with St. Martin's Press.
Library of Congress Catalog Card Number: 77-10308
ISBN: 0-380-46185-4

First Discus Printing, September, 1979

AVON TRADEMARK REG. U.S. PAT. OFF AND IN
OTHER COUNTRIES, MARCA REGISTRADA, HECHO EN
U.S.A.

Printed in the U.S.A.

# FOREWORD
## by Christmas Humphreys

This is an outstanding work almost unknown to the Western student of Buddhism, but it is so fresh and different in its handling of Buddhist principles that all may read it with advantage. In it they may see, perhaps for the first time, the principles of the oldest school of Buddhism, that of the Theravada as practised in Sri Lanka, Burma and Thailand, viewed by a mind learned in one of the later traditions, that of Tibet. These basic principles are to be found at the heart of every Buddhist school but developed and expressed to accord with the mentality of its members. There are those who may find them more readily acceptable when viewed from a new and unorthodox point of view.

The book was first published in English in 1939, by which date Mme David-Neel was already famous for her years of travel in Tibet in disguise, and for her profound knowledge of Tibetan culture and religion. It was therefore a surprise to many to find in the present work little mention of Tibet, but an independent and virile treatment of the Buddhist principles already becoming known to the Western mind. At this date I had myself already read a large proportion of the books on Buddhism available in London, and after the war was puzzled that such a fine work should have disappeared. One reason may have been that the public had expected another work on Tibet, even more exciting in its revelation of the peculiarities of Tibetan Buddhism.

This is no place for a life, however brief, of Mme David-Neel, but any biography yet to be written will describe how this small, resolute and highly unconventional Parisian made her way in disguise to Lasa, and spent several years there in Tibetan monasteries large and small, and in the high mountains for long periods alone. At this time there were few Western women with a knowledge of Tibetan Buddhism, none who had travelled the country for two years without her Western origin being discovered, and none before or since who so impressed the higher ranks of the Buddhist Order that she was, though a woman, given accommodation in Kum-bum, one of the most famous monasteries in the East. I was told when staying in Sikkim that not only did she hold her own with the most learned of the Lamas but in many cases added to their knowledge of their own speciality!

Then, with some eight books on Tibet to her credit (some never translated from the French), she added this to her collection. It deals with the principles of Theravada Buddhism, which then were well known in London, generally in the same series of formulae, such as the Three Signs of Being, the Four Noble Truths, the Eightfold Path, Karma and Rebirth and Nirvana. Mme David-Neel's approach to all this was unique. She clearly possessed a deeply learned mind which, in its handling of Buddhist principles, was nicely balanced between the cold, objective approach of the scholar and the more subjective attitude of the teacher who, as a practising Buddhist, was trying to present her profound convictions to the Western world.

After a brief description of the Buddha and his legendary life the writer passes to what the Buddha himself called the centre of his Teaching, 'suffering and the end of suffering'. There follows a brilliant and fresh analysis of the 'interdependent origins' of suffering, the twelve *nidanas* studied in every monastery in Tibet as the spokes of the Wheel of Life. Then comes the longest section in the book, the way out of suffering on the Eightfold Path which the All-Enlightened One had trodden to its end. Into all this are woven Tibetan parallels, with amusing stories used to give point to the principles described.

The chapter on Karma (she uses the neutral form Karman) goes deeper into the profound teachings of the Mahayana, including her own description of the Bardo Thödol, or the right method of conscious dying, made known to the West a few years earlier in Dr Evan-Wentz's *The Tibetan Book of the Dead*. The concluding chapter says what may be said of the Everest of consciousness, Nirvana.

My wife and I had the privilege of knowing Mme David-Neel well. We first met in 1936 in Nice, where she was staying with the Lama Yongden, who was the companion of her travels and her adopted son. We discussed at length her revelations on Tibetan Buddhism, and, finding that she took a keen interest in the growing Buddhist movement in Europe, discussed the potential dangers of making known in detail such doctrines as the Bardo Thödol. I have noted with interest the caution she uses in her description of the practice in the present volume. We last saw her in the Tibetan-style house which she had built for herself in Digne, in the Basse-Alpes, and were impressed to find her, at the age of 95, correcting proofs without spectacles in a room made dark against the summer sun. She died in 1969 at the age of 100.

I recommend this book to every Western student of Buddhism, whatever his school or place in what is still the widest and potentially most powerful field of human thought.

# INTRODUCTION

IS the study of Oriental philosophies of importance to us today? Is it reasonable, in the twentieth century, to give our attention to the theories held by our distant fore-runners in this world, while so many pressing problems demand our attention? Some will doubt it, holding that to expound once again the doctrines of the ancient philosophers of India or China is to waste precious time, or at least to spend it on a dilettante inquiry of no practical interest. I see the question otherwise.

When failure menaces a commercial undertaking, it is usual to make a careful inventory of its resources, so as to utilize them in order to prevent the threatened dis-aster. Is it not possible that a similar line of conduct will give equally useful results in another sphere, and does not the present situation of the world justify an inventory of the capital of ideas possessed by humanity?

Each philosophy, each religion which has arisen in the world, constitutes, in respect of its applications in the material order, an experience which we can turn to profit, either avoiding the errors into which our pre-decessors fell, and the harmful consequences resulting therefrom, or extracting from the teachings which they received some conclusions which had escaped them.

It is not a question of seeking precise directions from

masters who lived many centuries ago, and under conditions very different from ours. Any attempt to copy
them would result only in grotesque caricatures. On the
other hand, to recall certain fundamental precepts, certain
mental disciplines laid down by these masters, may be
profitable. The contrast existing between our habitual
opinions and those expressed by philosophers belonging
to other ages and to other countries than ours, ought to
help us to see more clearly whatever is worth preserving
and confirming in our stock of ideas and principles, and
what we should do well to reject. This, it would seem,
is an excellent object in itself, and even if the popularized
study of the philosophies which arose in India and in
China were to lead us no farther, we should have gained
something appreciable.

The present volume is the fruit of a collaboration of
many years, during which the help of Lama Yongden
has been invaluable to me, especially in collecting documents relating to Tibetan Buddhism, and in making
inquiries in the Tibetan monasteries.

The short description which we have given of the
doctrines and methods of Buddhism is, of course, very
far from including all of them. The immense Buddhist
literature, which, over and above the many canonical
works, includes thousands of commentaries and original
philosophic treatises, cannot be summed up in a book of
less than three hundred pages. My collaborator and I have
aimed only at showing the reader the more essential or
more striking points of the Buddhist theories and the

methods of mental training which derive from them. Familiarized with these, readers will be able, if the subject interests them, to study with advantage the more technical works which learned Orientalists have devoted to the separate examination of the various doctrines of Buddhism, or to certain phases of its philosophic development.

ALEXANDRA DAVID-NEEL

# I

## THE BUDDHA

WORKS devoted to the exposition of philosophical doctrines or religions usually begin with the biography of the founder. Most of these biographies are, however, largely if not wholly mythical. The piety of the average disciples has never failed to make the sages whom they celebrate perform such impossible deeds as are calculated to increase their renown in the eyes of the people, so that often enough within a few years of their death many of these masters are already seen to be transformed into mythological figures.

The Buddha was no exception. Archaeological discoveries have proved, beyond a doubt, his historical character, but apart from the legends we know very little about the circumstances of his life. We know the name he bore, Siddharta Gautama; the name of his mother, Mayâ; and that of his father, Suddhodana. The latter was a chieftain reigning over a small State lying at the feet of the Himalayas, in a district which today forms part of Nepal. One important point remains doubtful: did Suddhodana come of a pure Aryan stock, or was he, on the contrary, a member of the yellow race? Or had the ancestors of this petty prince, reigning over a frontier

State, endowed him, by marriages contracted between members of the white and yellow races, with a mixed heredity? The present inhabitants of Nepal—the Newars—are of yellow stock, but this does not justify any definite conclusion as to the racial characteristics of their predecessors on the same ground, twenty-five centuries ago.

Siddharta Gautama, who would have succeeded his father, renounced the succession to become *sannyâsin*. Such vocations were at that period by no means rare in India, and are of frequent occurrence even today.

It is difficult to find in any European language a word which is a correct translation of the term *sannyâsin*. The things represented by it does not exist in the West, and India seems to have the monopoly of it. *Sannyâsa* means 'renunciation', 'rejection'. The sannyâsin is in no way a monk; he is an independent ascetic who has 'rejected the three worlds': the world of men (ours), that of our ancestors (explained as signifying posthumous fame), and that of the gods (the bliss of Paradise).

The 'rejection' of the sannyâsin differs completely from the 'renunciation' of the Christian monk who abandons what he calls the *good things* of this world in order to win the joys of heaven, or from that of the mystic who burns with longing to unite himself with his God, and thinks to succeed by this surrender. The 'renunciation' of the monk has the character of a sacrifice, while he who dons the robe of the sannyâsin does it because he feels aversion, repugnance, for that which the great mass of men regard as the 'good things' and the 'joys' of the world. In the words once used by a sannyâsin while talking to me, 'he rejects them with satisfaction, as one would feel contentment in throwing off dirty and ragged clothing'. Sannyâsa is not a 'means' which one uses to attain an object; sannyâsa is an end in itself, a joyous liberation. Moreover, the sannyâsin is always freed from social and religious laws; freed from all bonds, he walks on a path which is known to him alone, and is responsible only to himself. He is, par excellence, an 'outsider'.

In India, the existence of sannyâsins goes back into remote antiquity. There is already mention, in the Rig Veda, of 'ascetics, clad in dirty yellow robes, who wander like the wind and have conquered the powers of the gods'. This evidently refers to the spiritual ancestors of those sannyâsins who, with no ties, possessing nothing, wander as their fancy leads them, 'free as the wind'. There are millions of such in India today, some of them highly venerable mystics or philosophers, and the majority fairly ordinary people, including numerous impostors.

In the time of the Buddha, ascetics, then known as *sramanas*, were generally independent mystics, who had sometimes received a sort of consecration from another sramana; but in many cases they omitted this ceremony, as did Siddharta Gautama. They might be disciples of such and such a master and live beside him, but they did not belong to any regularly constituted congregation. Between the sramanas of that period there was not the bond of a common faith. On the contrary, they were adepts of different doctrines, and were always free to change their opinions. Some among them even professed complete incredulity. Paradoxical as it seems to us, India has known materialistic mystics and atheistic ascetics, and one still meets them there today.

The organization of the religious order known as the *Sangha* was due to the disciples of the Buddha. Imitating them, about twelve centuries later, the celebrated Vedantic philosopher, Sankara acharya,[1] established the ten classes of orthodox Hindu sannyâsins, living in community. These have ended by monopolizing the title of sannyâsin, leaving to those of their brothers who are not organized in communities the more usual title of *sadhu*.

This explanation is intended merely to give some idea of the kind of religious life which Gautama had embraced before his spiritual illumination, and thus to throw some light on the attitude of mind which might have been his when he conceived his doctrine.

The ancient tradition, and the ancient texts inspired by it, tell us that Siddharta Gautama, although a husband and the father of a son, left his home and became a wandering *muni* (ascetic).

'The ascetic Gautama, in his youth, in the strength of early manhood, had his hair and beard shaved, took the yellow robe, and left his house to lead a homeless life.

[1] Sankara acharya is said to have been born in A.D. 788 and to have died in 820. However, according to some Indian authors he lived about the sixth or seventh century.

'It is a narrow servitude, the life in the home; freedom lies in abandoning the home; since he thought thus, he abandoned his home.'

Gautama thirsted for spiritual illumination, and ended by finding it; but not in the schools of the famous philosophers which he had at first entered as a pupil, nor yet in the ascetic practices so highly valued in India, despite his prolonged and cruel experience of them. It came to him when he sought it only in his own mind, when he was meditating in solitude, under a tree.

Then began for him a period of preaching which lasted for fifty years. The success of this preaching was considerable; Gautama attracted to himself numerous disciples who belonged, with a few exceptions, to the intellectual and social élite of India. Then, at the age of eighty-one, stricken with dysentery, and—a splendid example of energy—refusing to halt that he might receive attention because he was due to preach in a neighbouring city, he was prostrated by sickness beside the road which he was following in the company of several of his disciples.

According to the Pâli texts which describe his end, he stopped for the first time, lying down for a moment on the ground, and then, making an effort, he set off again. But the old Master had no strength left. A little farther on, at his request, his cousin and disciple Ananda took off his cloak and spread it out at the foot of a little grove formed by three sandalwood trees.

'Fold my cloak, I pray thee, Ananda, and put it under me.'

Knowing how hard it is for most men to free themselves from all sentimental devotion, knowing their need of gods conceived in their own image, or of deified human masters, knowing their inability to live the spiritual life in solitude, Gautama spoke to his cousin:

'It may be, Ananda, that this thought may arise in some of you: The word of the Master is no more; we no longer have a Master.

'It is not thus that you should think. The doctrine and the discipline which I have taught you shall be your Master when I am no longer with you.'

Then, as a final exhortation to those around him: 'Hear me. I say to you that dissolution is inherent in all formations. Work diligently for your deliverance!'

And the Buddha was for ever silent. But, as he had just said, he left an immortal Master behind him, the Doctrine and the Rules which he had laid down; and among the rules of conduct was this:

'Be a torch unto yourselves. Be a refuge unto yourselves. Let truth be your torch and your refuge, and seek no other. And he who either now or after I have gone shall be his own torch and his own refuge, he who shall take the truth as his torch and his refuge shall be my true disciple, who knows what he should rightfully do.' (Parinibbâna Sutta.)

Such a precept, by its virile character, gives Buddhism actuality in all ages.

The very simple circumstances of the life and death of the Buddha, as tradition has remembered them, apart from the 'embellishments' of legend, are authentic enough. It is probable that everything happened as we are told, or approximately so. But this fact, which would be of primary importance in a religion centred in the person of its founder, is of no great significance to the Buddhist. What matters, we are told, are the facts which this doctrine brings to our notice, so that we can deduce from them the practical consequences which they involve.

'Whether Buddhas appear or whether they do not appear, one fact remains: that all aggregations of elements are impermanent. This fact a Buddha discovers and grasps, and when he has discovered and grasped it, he announces it, publishes it, proclaims it, minutely explains it and makes it clear.' (Anguttara-Nikâya.)

The same thing is repeated concerning the 'suffering' inherent in all aggregates of elements, and the absence of an 'ego', non-compounded and lasting, within these aggregates.

The Buddha did not claim that he had uttered a revelation of a supernatural order; he never propagated any dogma; he never appealed to faith. He simply offered to men, for their examination, a method which it would be well for them to utilize for their own benefit, and of which the declared aim is the Destruction of Suffering.

# II

# THE BASIS OF THE BUDDHIST DOCTRINE

AS in the case of the story of the Buddha's life, so as regards his teaching, we can grasp only a few fundamental features with any certainty. Just as the Gospels which are now read by the faithful are accepted as having been compiled long after the death of Jesus, and give us only an exposition of the traditions and opinions which were current among Christians at the time of this compilation, so the doctrines which we find in the Buddhist canonical books, even in the most ancient of them, are merely the doctrines professed by the editors of these scriptures and their contemporaries, several centuries after the death of the Buddha.

Do these teachings differ from those laid down by the Master? We may suppose that in course of time the original doctrine underwent certain modifications; such a process is usual and normal, but it would be rash to attempt to indicate the nature of these modifications. It would be even less reasonable to state that, on fundamental questions, Siddharta Gautama held opinions opposed to those which are the basis of the Buddhist doctrine as delivered to us in what are considered to be the oldest texts. How should we set about proving the existence of a 'more authentic' teaching, of which no documentary record exists?

In any case, all discussions of this kind are useless. According to the explicit statement of the canonical texts, the doctrine does not derive any authority from the person of the teacher; it claims to be based on facts. It is, then, open to us to verify the statements made to us and prove whether they are true or not.

Although Buddhist literature includes an enormous number of works, and although Buddhist authors speak poetically of an 'ocean of doctrine', all this literature is really nothing more than a gigantic commentary, constantly amplified in the course of the centuries, on a very simple doctrine, and a few directions, the whole of which can be shown on a couple of pages, as in the table on pages 24–25.

On the thesis represented in this table, thousands of thinkers during the last twenty-five centuries have exercised their reasoning powers and their imagination. Consequently, innumerable theories have been grafted on to it, which sometimes differ considerably from the fundamental ideas of which they profess to be the development, and are even, in some cases, in flat contradiction to them.

In order to bolster up this new Buddhism, elaborated on the margin of the older, more rational doctrine, many authors have put their own ideas in the mouth of the Buddha, in those speeches which he is supposed to have

## The Doctrine of the Buddha:

| SUFFERING | THE CAUSE OF SUFFERING | THE CESSATION OF SUFFERING |
|---|---|---|
| This can be summarized in two definitions.<br><br>1. To be in contact with that for which one feels aversion.<br><br>2. To be separated from that for which one feels attraction, or, in other words, not to possess what one desires. | It is *Ignorance*, basis of the eleven other links of the Chain of Interdependent Origins.<br><br>These eleven links may be arranged under three heads:<br><br>1. *Ignorance.*<br>2. *Desire*, which arises from Ignorance.<br>3. *Action*, which follows Desire, as a means of satisfying it.<br><br>As a consequence of the sensations experienced in accomplishing the action, new desires arise.<br><br>(*a*) A desire to feel again the same sensations, if the action has caused sensations of an agreeable kind.<br><br>(*b*) A desire to avoid these same sensations, if the action has caused sensations of a disagreeable kind.<br><br>This new desire urges us to the accomplishment of new actions—either to induce the desired sensations, or to prevent the repetition of disagreeable sensations.<br><br>This action, in its turn, produces sensations which, as before, give rise to desires, and the concatenation of actions, sensations, and desires, giving rise to new actions, continues to infinity, so long as *Ignorance* exists. | It is the destruction of *Ignorance* which produces the destruction of *Desire*.<br><br>The *Desire* having ceased to exist, the urge to *action* no longer arises.<br><br>*Action* no longer taking place, the sensations resulting from its accomplishment no longer arise, and the *desires*, of which these sensations are the source, no longer arise.<br><br>The cause having ceased to exist, the revolution of the Chain of Interdependent Origins also ceases. |

# The Four Truths

---

---

It consists in a programme of mental training, which may be summed up as follows:

## Acquisition of Right Views

These comprise a perfect understanding of:

| The Three General Characteristics | The Four Truths |
| --- | --- |
| The impermanence of all aggregates | Suffering |
| The suffering inherent in all aggregates | Its cause |
| | Its cessation |
| The absence of an *ego* in all aggregates | The Way which leads to this cessation |

Having acquired *Right Views*, one knows the real nature of the objects composing the external world, and the real nature of oneself. Possessing this knowledge, one ceases to desire, out of delusion, that which produces suffering, and to reject that which produces happiness.

One practises an enlightened *Morality*, in the highest sense of the word. This does not consist in passive obedience to a code imposed by a God or by any other external power. Having oneself recognized perfectly those acts which it is good to perform, and those from which, for one's own benefit and for that of others, one should abstain, one's conduct conforms to the knowledge which one has acquired on this subject.

The *Means* of acquiring *Right Views* are:

*Perfect Attention*, which comprises: Study; analysis of the perceptions, the sensations, the states of consciousness, of all the operations of the mind and of the physical activity which corresponds with them; observation; reflection.

*Perfect Meditation*, comprising concentration of mind; a physical and psychical education which aims at producing mental and bodily calm, and acuteness of the senses (the mind counting as sixth sense), and awakening new perceptions, thus enabling the mind to extend the field of its investigations.

made before mythical audiences of gods and others. Nevertheless, even in these imaginary discourses the subjects discussed always, directly or indirectly, relate to one of the fundamental points shown in the above table. From this one is entitled to conclude that these points do, in fact, constitute the basis of Buddhist doctrine, and that the earliest disciples of Gautama probably received them directly from their Master.

It is indispensable that any study of Buddhism should begin with the profound consideration of the doctrine here presented in tabular form, so as to show the interrelation of its different teachings. Without a thorough knowledge of this doctrine, the study of the Buddhist writers, especially of the Mahâyânist philosophers, is likely to produce confusion in the reader's mind and to give him quite erroneous notions of the real ideas of these authors.

# III

# SUFFERING AND THE SUPPRESSION OF SUFFERING

THE Buddhist doctrine is founded on the existence of suffering; it is suffering that gives it its *raison d'être*, and it is suffering that is proposed, before all, and insistently, as the subject of our meditations. It is this, no doubt, that has given Buddhism the reputation of a school of pessimism. However, when Buddhism begins its teaching by establishing the existence of suffering, it simply registers a fact which any reasonable man is bound to admit.

Briefly, there are four possible attitudes in respect of suffering:

(1) The denial, in the face of all evidence, of its existence.

(2) Passive resignation, the acceptance of a state of things which one considers inevitable.

(3) The 'camouflage' of suffering by the help of pompous sophistries, or by gratuitously attaching to it such virtues and transcendent aims as one thinks may ennoble it or diminish its bitterness.

(4) The war against suffering, accompanied by faith in the possibility of overcoming it.

The fourth attitude is that adopted by Buddhism.

It is enough to glance at the foregoing table to see that, immediately after drawing our attention to the fact of the existence of suffering, Buddhism at once directs it toward an entirely practical aim: to 'deliverance from suffering.'

This table shows us, also, the real character of the Buddhist doctrine. We are not confronted with a revelation concerning the origin of the world and the nature of the First Cause. There is no mention of a Supreme Divinity, nor any promise of superhuman aid for suffering humanity.

We have before us a simple programme, the plan for a sort of intellectual battle which man must fight alone, and from which he is told that he can emerge victorious by relying on his own powers.

The invention of this fourfold programme, known as the 'Four Truths', is attributed to the Buddha; it is based on his own conduct as described by tradition.

The Buddha, as described for us by tradition, had thoroughly grasped the wretched nature of the existence of all beings subject to illness, old age, and death, and to all the kinds of suffering which accompany 'contact with that for which one feels aversion—losing touch with, or separation from, that which one loves—failure to obtain that which one desires'. Nevertheless, when considering this distressing outlook, Gautama did not give way to useless despair. In leaving his home, in breaking the social and family ties which bound him, he did not obey, as many Hindus have done, a simple mystical impulse; he began a struggle.

Alone, armed only with his understanding, he was going to seek the way out which would allow of escape from the suffering inseparably bound up with all individual existence. He would seek to cross the rushing torrent of perpetual formations and dissolutions, the *samsâra*; the eternal circle, the infinite whirlpool, the idea of which haunted the philosophers of his country, and which popular beliefs illustrated by transmigrations and puerile metempsychoses. He would attempt this titanic escape, not for his own salvation alone, but also for that of the mass of human beings whose pitiable distress he had perceived with the eyes of the Sage.

He did not think of appealing for help for them, or for himself. What could the gods do? Their celestial realms, however splendid they may be, and their life, however glorious one may imagine it, are dominated by the same laws of decrepitude and dissolution as ours. They are our giant brothers, our sublime brothers; perhaps redoubtable tyrants, perhaps compassionate protectors; but they have in no way saved the world from suffering; they have not even freed themselves from it.

What a paltry ideal is that of rebirth in one of those celestial hostelries, the *svargas*![1] To know, to understand, to cross to the 'other shore' whence one perceives another aspect of phenomena, where turmoil changes into serenity, where the changeless emerges from the transitory; is such a victory possible for man? The

[1] The *svargas* are the various paradises, the dwellings of the gods.

Buddha thought so, and triumphantly he turns to us to teach us how to traverse the ocean of sorrowful existence, to give 'to the world sunk in the shadows of ignorance and disquiet, the splendid light of the highest knowledge'. (Lalita Vistara.)

Whatever opinion one may hold as to the singularity of such an enterprise, one must admit that the example of this heroic combat, for those who meditate on it, is more likely to lead to useful activity than to incline them toward indolence.

Some have thought that the suffering which Buddhism envisages has nothing in common with the ordinary sorrows and pains of life; that it is a sort of metaphysical suffering; the *Weltschmerz* of German philosophy. One can hardly escape the conclusion that a thinker of the Buddha's profundity must, in his perception of suffering, have outgrown the limits of trivial material or moral suffering; yet it was of these only that he spoke, avoiding everything that might have tended to involve teaching in metaphysical speculations.

'Old age is suffering, illness is suffering, death is suffering, being in contact with that which one dislikes is suffering, being separated from that which one likes is suffering, failure to realize one's desire is suffering.'

The list can easily be reduced to the two points shown in our table, for old age, illness, and death are 'suffering' because we dislike them.

On the other hand, if contact with that which one dislikes, separation from that which one likes, nonrealization of one's desires, can include subtle moral sufferings, it is no less clear that all the more sordid pains of daily life fall, naturally, into one or other of these three categories.

To put an end to *all* suffering is evidently the final aim which Buddhism proposes to attain; in the meantime it encourages us to pursue and destroy the pains with which we find ourselves in contact, whether they afflict ourselves, or whether we see them afflicting others. Buddhist ethics, which are a sort of spiritual hygiene, tend to destroy in us the causes of suffering inflicted on others, while the fundamental teaching of Buddhism: 'All suffering springs from ignorance', and the obligation laid upon its followers to endeavour to acquire—in all domains—correct views, attacks the causes of our own sufferings.

With regard to the Buddha so often depicted by Western writers as a nonchalant dreamer, an elegant nihilist, scorning effort, we can regard him as a myth. Buddhist tradition has no record of such a person. The Sage who gave fifty years of his life to preaching his doctrine, and then, over eighty years of age, died, when still active, falling beside the road which he was following on foot, on the way to expound his teaching to new listeners, has no resemblance to the anaemic, disillusioned man whom such writers had sometimes attempted to substitute for him.

In reality, if we consider its essential principles, Buddhism is a school of Stoic energy, of unwearying perseverance and singular audacity, the object of which is the training of 'warriors' to attack suffering.

'Warriors, warriors we call ourselves. We fight for splendid virtue, for high endeavour, for sublime wisdom, therefore we call ourselves warriors.' (Anguttara Nikâya.)

And according to Buddhism, the conquest of Wisdom which, for it, is indissolubly bound up with Knowledge, leads infallibly to the destruction of suffering. But how can the will to fight suffering come to us if we do not give serious attention to it, if in the interval between two pains we forget, in a moment of pleasure, that we suffered yesterday, and that we may again suffer to-morrow? Or again, if selfishly enjoying this respite, we remain indifferent to the sufferings of others, without understanding that so long as the causes which produce sorrow exist it may come to us in our turn?

For these reasons Buddhism first of all draws our attention to suffering. Not, as we have already seen, in order to drive us to despair, but in order to make us discern, in all its forms, beneath all its disguises, the enemy which we have to fight.

# IV

# INTERDEPENDENT ORIGINS

LONG before the time of the Buddha, the idea of cause and effect, that of action followed by its fruits, was general among the intellectuals of India. Gautama as a child, and later as a young man, would not have learned from his instructors the doctrine of one unique god, an all-powerful deity, the creator and lord of the world, ordering as he chose the destiny of creatures and of things. He would more probably have heard them rendering the doctrine which was afterwards to become the *credo* of orthodox Buddhism: 'All phenomena arise from a cause.' An impersonal cause, it must be understood, inherent in the very nature of things, and not the conscious will of a living being. Imbued with this doctrine, and having conceived the project of 'putting an end to suffering', Gautama had, quite naturally, to seek for the cause of suffering.

We know that he first made inquiries of several renowned philosophers. Tradition has preserved for us the names of two among them, Alara Kalama and Rudraka Ramaputra, who lived, respectively, at Vaisali and Rajagriha, but it is certain that Gautama spent some time with other masters.

There were then, as there are today in India, many small groups of disciples following philosophical studies under the direction of the master of their choice, and devoting themselves, under his guidance, to psychic exercises. Subtle orators and ingenious inventors of abstruse theories held their schools in gardens, or on the borders of the forest near the towns, while farther away, and living in solitude, were rationalistic mystics, materialistic magicians, and atheistical hermits—a whole world of characters disconcerting to our Western mentality. One and all disappointed Gautama. He did not find among them the answer which he sought.

In accordance with the ideas current in India at the time—and they are still held by many—the future Buddha then sought to develop his spiritual faculties by mortification. This method was not successful. The self-inflicted torments and prolonged fasts had no result beyond reducing him to a state of excessive weakness which brought him to the verge of death. This lesson was useful to Gautama, who afterwards enabled his disciples to profit by it, forbidding them, equally with sensuality, austerities which ruin the health and reduce the vigour of the mind. Having regained his strength, the determined seeker, always obsessed by the eternal drama of life and death, by the spectacle of the suffering inherent in all existence, resumed his meditations.

How interesting it would have been to possess a diary, written by the Master's hand, recording the sequence of ideas which led him to conceive this chain of twelve links of interdependent causes, which seemed to him to constitute the 'Cause of Suffering'. Unfortunately we have to content ourselves with what his biographers have to tell us about it, and their narratives are particularly concise.

It would be a mistake to imagine that Siddharta Gautama was the only person in India to seek for the cause of suffering. This problem, closely bound up with that of the origin of living beings, and the causes which made them what they are, subject to decrepitude and to death, had already occupied Hindu philosophers several centuries before the birth of the future Buddha. The oldest Upanishads, handed down orally for perhaps two hundred years before Gautama began his search, contain evidence—in the written versions which were later made of them—of the existence of such preoccupations among the intellectual aristocracy of the Brahmins and the Kshattriyas. In a Buddhist Sutta, the Brahmâjala Sutta, the Buddha is reported to have described sixty-two different schools of philosophy, upholding different views regarding the ego and the world, their origin, their nature, etc. While receiving with due reserve the information furnished by documents based merely on tradition, we can have no doubt that the ideas of Siddharta Gautama were developed in an environment in which philosophic doctrines abounded. Hence, without any deliberate borrowing, the Buddha might well have included in his doctrine certain theories forming part of a common fund, modifying them or associating them with other theories which were the fruit of his own meditations.

However this may be, the 'Cause of Suffering' is described by Buddhism in the form of a process in twelve stages, known as *Pratîtyasamûtpâda*.[1] According to Professor Stcherbatsky, the expression *pratîtyasamûtpâda* means 'interdependent origins' or 'combined and dependent origins'. Professor La Vallée Poussin explains it as 'appearance or production of beings as the result of causes and conditions'.

The theory of the 'Twelve Interdependent Origins' lies at the root of Buddhist doctrine. It is, as shown in the table included in Chapter II, in direct relation with the 'Four Truths' on which Buddhism is based, and is an inseparable part of them. It results from this that all Buddhist authors, since the Buddhist Canon was first reduced to writing, down to the present day, have incessantly, and in many different fashions, studied, explained, and commented upon this series of causes which are shown to be the producers of suffering.

We are told that in the mind of Gautama, meditating at the foot of a tree, there suddenly arose the 'vision' of the interdependent origins or productions.

Once more he asked himself:

What is it that causes old age, death, illness, suffering, and sorrow? Or, more literally: What is it which must exist in order that old age, death, etc. . . . should exist? He answered his own question: It is birth—the fact of

[1] In Pali: *Paticcasamuppada*.

being born—which causes the advent of old age, death, illness, pain, and sorrow.

What is it that must exist in order that birth should be produced ?—Becoming.

In many Buddhist writings—translations of the original texts, or written directly in Western languages—we find, at this point, the word *existence* instead of *becoming*, and the former term, although justified if one understands the meaning which the Buddhists attribute to it, leads to some confusion. What the texts mean by the word *bhava* is existence in the form of movement, the continual appearance of successive phenomena, in a word: *becoming*. The word *sat* which we encounter in the terminology of the Vedanta, where it signifies the absolute being, the unique existence, is unknown in Buddhism.

Comprehending existence thus, as the active form of a continual becoming, we shall understand more clearly the explanation given by the Buddha to Ananda, which is recorded in the Maha-Nidana Sutta of the Digha Nikaya:

'I have said that birth depended on existence. This should be understood as follows: Suppose, Ananda, that there was absolutely no existence for anyone, of any kind; neither existence in the world of desire, nor existence in the world of pure form, nor existence in the world without form[1]; if there were nowhere any existence, existence having entirely ceased, would birth produce itself ? (Would there be birth ?)'

---

[1] Kâma lôka, Rupa lôka, Arûpa lôka: The three worlds, or condition, of existence recognized by Buddhists.

'No, Venerable One.'

'Thus existence is the cause, the occasion, the origin of birth; birth depends on it.'

With existence (becoming) we reach the second article of the enumeration of interdependent origins. This continues as follows:

'What is it which must exist so that there may be "becoming"?'

'The action of seizing, drawing to one's self.'

'What is it which must exist for this grasping to take place?'

'Thirst.' (Desire.)

'What is it which must exist for the "thirst" to arise?'

'Sensation.'

'What is it which must exist to produce "sensation"?'

'Contact.'

'What is it which must exist for there to be "contact"?'

'The senses and their objects.'

These senses are six in number for the Buddhists, who consider the mind as a sixth sense whose concern is with ideas.

'What is it which must exist for the senses to exist?'

'The material body and the mind.'[1]

'What is it which must exist in order that body and mind (the realm of material form and that of mental form) shall exist?'

'Consciousness.'

---

[1] This inseparable couple is technically termed, in Buddhism: *Name and Form*. Name includes the various activities which constitute the 'mental'.

'What is it which must exist for this Consciousness to exist?'

'Mental formations or creations in general.'

'What is it which must exist for these mental formations to exist?'

'Ignorance.'

The canonical Scriptures tell us that the Buddha, having reached this point, then reviewed this process in the reverse direction:

Ignorance not existing—the mental formations do not exist.

The mental formations not existing—consciousness does not exist.

Consciousness not existing—the material body and the mind do not exist.

The material body and the mind not existing—the six senses do not exist.

The six senses not existing—contact does not exist. (Does not take place.)

Contact not existing—sensation does not exist (Is not produced.)

Sensation not existing—thirst (desire) does not exist. (Is not produced.)

Thirst (desire) not existing—grasping (the action of seizing, drawing to one's self) does not exist.

Grasping not existing—existence (becoming) does not exist. (Is not produced.)

Existence (becoming) not existing—birth does not exist. (Is not produced.)

Birth not existing—old age, death, illness, pain, do not exist. (Are not produced.)

Thus ceases all this mass of suffering.

Presented in this way, this enumeration appears to have for its only object to teach us how not to be reborn[1] and to avoid by this means the evils inherent in all life and the inevitable death which ends it. Such is, actually, the manner in which the Theravadin Buddhists generally understand the *pratîtyasamûtpâda*.

The school of philosophy of the Theravadins is more generally known under the name of *Hinayâna*. Hinayâna means 'Lesser Vehicle' or 'Lower Vehicle', and in the picturesque language of the East this word 'vehicle' means, in this case, a body of doctrine and practical instruction calculated to lead the faithful towards knowledge, spiritual illumination, and the cessation of suffering. It goes without saying that it was not the adepts of this school—which includes several sects—who gave the doctrines which they follow the humiliating denomination of 'lesser' or 'lower'. This epithet was applied to them, in scorn, by their philosophical opponents, who named their own doctrines *Mahâyâna*, the 'Great Vehicle', in the sense of superiority, not of size.

The Theravadins (Hinayânists) say that the development of the 'Twelve Origins' extends over three suc-

---

[1] It is perhaps needless to say that Buddhists, like Hindus, believe in a plurality of lives. This fact is well known.

cessive lives, our previous life, our present life, and our future life. As follows:

| Previous life | 1. Ignorance<br>2. Mental formations or creations, volitions, etc. | Process of Action |
|---|---|---|
| Present life | 3. Consciousness<br>4. Body and Mind<br>5. Six organs of sense and their objects<br>6. Contact<br>7. Sensation | Process of Rebirth |
| | 8. Thirst (Desire)<br>9. Grasping (attachment, drawing to one's self)<br>10. 'Becoming' (existence) | Process of Action |
| Future life | 11. Rebirth<br>12. Decrepitude and Death | Process of Rebirth |

The successive rebirths are shown in this scheme as being the result of two alternate processes.

(1) *Process of Action*, consisting in mental activity exercised under the influence of ignorance. This activity shows itself by Desire, by the act of drawing to one's self, of seizing in thought, by attachment. 'Becoming,' or existence in the form of mental and physical acts, follows.

(1) *Process of Rebirth*, rebirth being the consequence of desire and attachment, and bringing with it consciousness, body and mind, the six senses, contact and sensation.

(3) *Process of Action*: desire, attachment, etc., arising as a result of existence.

(*a*) of sensation.

(*b*) of contact which produces sensation.

(*c*) of the six senses through the medium of which contact takes place.

(*d*) of the body and mind without which the six senses would not exist.

(*e*) of consciousness influenced by ignorance, which causes wrong interpretations of the information given by the senses, and gives rise to desires tending toward grasping, attachment, etc., in short, toward a new

(4) *Process of Rebirth*, leading, like the former rebirths, to decrepitude and death.

And thus revolves the round of successive lives.

Those Buddhists who adhere to the particular conception of the *pratîtyasamûtpâda* which has just been explained above, generally conceive these successive lives in the form of 'series' (santâna) of successive moments of consciousness. According to them, each of these 'series' constitutes an autonomous line, which proceeds upon its way, and whose unknowable origin is lost in the mists of time. It is to these 'series' that the Hinayânists apply the declaration attributed to the Buddha: 'Unknowable is the beginning of beings enwrapped in ignorance, whom desire leads to continued rebirth.' According to them, these 'series', lacking any perceptible beginning, can have an end. This end consists in the cessation of the activity of the 'series', and this cessation is regarded as *nirvâna*.

Faithful to the doctrine which denies the existence of the ego, a doctrine professed—at least in theory—by all Buddhists, the adherents to the theory of the 'series' do not fail to affirm that the 'series' is a simple process of moments of consciousness within which no individual, no 'ego' exists. However, in spite of their explanations, we cannot fail to see a disguised form of the ego in a 'series' which traverses the ages as an isolated process.

After all, is such an isolation in agreement with the operation of the *pratîtyasamûtpâda*, and is it possible?

The operation of the *pratîtyasamûtpâda* implies the connection of the moments of consciousness with external objects. Consciousness arises because it has been produced by sensations, and sensations are produced by contact.

Now the nature of the contact determines the nature of the sensation which it produces, and, in its turn, the nature of the sensation determines the nature of the moment of consciousness which follows. So, by virtue of the contact, an external influence is acting on the 'series', and therefore this can no longer be said to be autonomous, for it carries, joined to itself, the effects of its contact with another 'series'. Such contacts—conscious or unconscious—take place several times in each minute, and consequently we are led to consider the 'series' as intimately related to one another, as dependent upon one another, which amounts to saying that no real, continuous, isolated 'series' exist.[1]

When one studies the *pratîtyasamûtpâda*, one should not consider the twelve articles which compose it as being a succession of events which follow each other in the order given. The co-existence of some of them is constant; *ignorance* is always present, for if it should disappear the eleven other 'origins' would equally disappear. *Body and mind* and the *senses*, also, cannot fail to be present, for they are necessary to the existence of other links of the chain. *Contact* and *sensation* postulate the existence of *senses* and of objects. Desire, the *act of seizing* a longed-for object, or the act of rejecting an object for which one feels aversion, brings into play *consciousness*, which has formed a judgement as a result of the *sensation* felt. *Desire*, the *act of seizing*, *attachment*, are themselves a source of *sensations* which *consciousness* registers, and on which it exercises its activity. These associations, this constant co-operation of interdependent origins, conditioned and co-ordinated, are in fact that which constitutes the process of action and the process of rebirth.

The succession of these processes, shown as including three lives (past, present, and future) is difficult to accept. In reality, it is from one moment to the next that the whole revolution of *pratîtyasamûtpâda* is produced.

Among the adepts of the Mahâyâna sect we find an interesting diversity of interpretations of the chain of

[1] See in Chapter VI the parable of the fires and the sparks.

'interdependent origins'. Over and above the classic commentaries of the famous doctors of the 'Great Vehicle', many special ways of conceiving the working of *pratítyasamûtpâda* are to be noted among contemporary mystics and philosophers.

According to certain Tibetans, the expression *ignorance*, which heads the list of 'origins', may be taken as 'unconsciousness' (unawareness). Regarded in this light, the interdependent origins which, according to the Theravadins (Hinayânists) are concerned solely with living beings, and especially with men, enlarge their field of action, which then includes the whole universe.

*Birth* takes the general sense of arising, whatever it may be that arises, in the realm of matter or in that of the mind.

*Desire* (thirst) no longer necessarily depends on the *consciousness* forming a judgement on the sensation experienced. It may emanate from the subconscious, and manifest itself as a spontaneous impulse arising from a reaction due to the nature of the elements composing the impermanent aggregate which appears to us as a 'person' or a 'thing'. It may even, they say, proceed simply from the instinct of preservation which obscurely demands the aliments necessary for the continued existence of the existing 'group', whatever may be the nature of this latter. *Desire, thirst for existence*, show themselves in the plant as in the animal. It is further said that *Desire, grasping*, can also connote attractions of a natural order, such as the action of a magnet.[1]

---

[1] In Tibetan: *Khan len rdo*, 'Stone needle taker'. Natural magnet.

In studying the theory of the twelve origins, one must bear in mind that Buddhism sees, in everything, groups or assemblages. The origin indicated—whether it be ignorance, desire, or no matter which of the other origins included in the *pratîtyasamûtpâda*—is not a unit. The name which is given us covers a group of constituent elements, and this group is not stable; it changes with bewildering rapidity. To object at this point that however infinitesimal may be its duration in time, one feels only *one* desire, and one thinks only *one* thought at any one moment, would be beside the point. Even though some deny the fact that the same moment cannot be occupied by several simultaneous thoughts or desires— an opinion which I leave to them to justify—it must be understood, here, that the desire, the thought, or what not, is the product of multiple causes, and contains in itself the various elements which it received from its parentage. The question, as it is seen by some authors of commentaries on the *pratîtyasamûtpâda*—among others, by a graduate of Dérgé with whom I discussed it—bears some relation to the fact that two bodies cannot occupy the same point in space. My interlocutor brushed aside all argument on this subject, saying: A thousand things exist in that which you see as a *single* thing, and occupy the same space. All the past phenomena which produced the form and the mind which you call a *géchès* (a graduate of a monastic university)—he meant by this himself—are, with this *géchès*, sitting on a chair, in this room. Expressing this idea more in accordance with Western mentality,

one might say that all that has gone to make up the
heredity of an individual is present in the space occupied
by him.

When one knows—we are told—that phenomena arise
in dependence on causes and disappear in dependence on
causes; when one knows how, in the world, everything
forms and dissolves, the ordinary conceptions of existence
and non-existence disappear. Or again: 'The world is
accustomed to cling to a duality, *being* and *non-being*.
But for him who perceives, with wisdom, how things
are produced and disappear in the world, there is neither
*being* nor *non-being*.'

Nothing exists *in itself*, for every phenomenon is the
product of causes, and nothing can be destroyed, since it,
in its turn, becomes a cause, after having been an effect.—
However, there are those who deny this last statement.

It is to be noted that with the Hinayânists, as with the
Mahâyânists, the theory of *pratîtyasamûtpâda* excludes any
idea of a First Cause, of God the Creator, and of an
'ego' which transmigrates. The canonical books abound
in statements on this point.

'No one,' we are told, 'accomplishes the action, no one
experiences the results, only the succession of actions and
their results revolves in a continual cycle, like the "round"
of the tree and the seed, and no one can say when it
began. It is equally impossible to perceive when, in the
course of future births, actions and results will cease to
succeed one another.'

We must note that there is here no question of the prolongation of *series* of autonomous lines of process, which are destined to finish in isolation on attaining Nirvâna. This passage seems rather to depict a movement which concerns the whole universe. 'Those who do not discern this concatenation believe in the existence of an ego; some hold it to be eternal, others declare it to be perishable, and from these two opinions arise many contradictory theories.'

'One cannot find the effect in the action, nor the action in the effect, yet no effect exists without the existence of an action. No reserve of fire exists in the combustible, nor elsewhere, outside of it; yet without combustible there is no fire. Similarly, we cannot find the effect in the action, nor outside it; actions exist apart from their effects, and effects exist separately from actions, but the effects come to pass as the results of actions.'

'The endless round of Births is not caused by any god, but the elements produced by the causes and the materials which constitute beings follow their course. A "round" of action, a "round" of effects, birth arising from action, so turns and turns the world.'

'When a disciple,' it is stated, 'has grasped in this way this round of action and its results (which present themselves in the form of new actions) he understands that body and mind exist in dependence on causes. He understands, then, that the "groups" of constituent elements—which we call beings, persons—which have arisen in the past on account of actions accomplished, have perished, but that, as the result of actions accomplished by these 'groups', other 'groups', other beings, have arisen. Not one of the elements which were found in the old 'groups' has transmigrated from the previous existence into this one, and not one element of the present 'groups' will pass into the next existence.'

'To believe that he who performs an action is the same as he who will reap its fruit is an extreme opinion. To believe that he who performs an action and he who reaps its fruit are two completely different persons is another extreme opinion. The Buddha avoided these two extremes and declared: "Ignorance existing, the mental formations (the 'creations') exist—mental formations existing, consciousness exists, etc.'[1] (See the list of the twelve interdependent origins given above.)

Whatever may be the interpretation given to the *pratîtyasamûtpâda*, the ignorance mentioned at the head of the list of 'origins' is never taken as a primary cause of a metaphysical order. The word is generally accepted in its simplest meaning: ignorance = not to know. 'It is not permissible to attribute to the Buddhist Avidya a cosmic and metaphysical character; it is a psychological factor, the state of him who is ignorant,' writes Professor de La Vallée Poussin.

Nevertheless, some Buddhists have conceived the character of this ignorance to be positive rather than negative, making ignorance not only the absence of knowledge, but the opposite of knowledge—

[1] From the Visuddhi Magga.

that is to say, error, false knowledge, obscured and
defiled.

Their theory finds support in the terms of the
*pratîtyasamûtpâda* itself. If one thing is the origin of
another, it is evident that this first thing is not just pure
non-existence; that it has something positive about it,
capable of action. We are told that *ignorance* consists in
not knowing the Four Truths, the basis of Buddhism,
and, in consequence, the chain of interdependent Origins
(excluding the existence of an ego) which corresponds
to the Second Truth, 'The Cause of Suffering'. However,
in order that it may engender *mental formations*, ignorance
must be more than the passivity of pure not-knowing; it
must become *knowledge*, but false knowledge, error.

He who is ignorant of the chain of interdependent
origins, who is ignorant that the 'person' is an aggregate
of unstable elements—such a one does not remain inert.
He holds *views*. The sport of illusion, he believes in the
existence of a permanent, uncompounded 'ego'; he
imagines that a prime Cause exists, creating and guiding
the world, and he personifies it, he makes a gigantic
'ego' of it. Thus his lack of knowledge is transformed into
a false idea, and becomes the origin of mental acts (formations, volitions) which are related to it and share its
falsity.

We are also told that *ignorance* is ignorance of the origin
and the end of the 'group' constituting the person. Again,
ignorance consists in believing that which is transitory to
be eternal, or that which is painful to be pleasant.

Ignorance, then, is not only lack of knowledge, but wrong knowledge; it is that which hides things and prevents one from seeing them as they are in reality.

Understanding *ignorance* in this way, it becomes less difficult to grasp the basic idea of the *pratîtyasamûtpâda* which makes *ignorance*, not a veritable initial origin, a starting-point, but an origin among other origins, itself conditioned by *that which exists because ignorance exists*, but without whose existence ignorance itself would not exist either.

Here, we must not forget, we are dealing with a cycle, a 'round', and not a straight line of filiation.

We cannot properly speak of antecedents of *ignorance*, for in all states of existence which it is possible for us to perceive, ignorance is present. The canonical texts definitely state that ignorance is without any perceptible beginning, but the existence of ignorance and its continuity are said to depend on 'aliments', which, if they ceased to exist, would thereby bring about the cessation of ignorance. It is precisely to the suppression of these 'aliments' that the disciple desirous of attaining to spiritual Illumination applies himself.

Buddhist authors vary slightly in enunciating the bases of ignorance, but the most usual classification is as follows:

(1) Lack of mastery over our senses. (2) Unconsciousness of impressions experienced. (3) Inattention; Attention wrongly directed; Thoughtlessness. (4) Incredulity as regards the Four Truths and the teachings which follow from them. (5) Lack of knowledge of the Doctrine of

the Four Truths, which one has not heard expounded.
(6) Non-association with enlightened people who have
reached the goal of the Doctrine.

As a result of one or more of these facts, harmful
actions are committed by the body and mind and in
speech.

These harmful actions nourish covetousness, wickedness, indolence, pride, and doubt (concerning the Four
Truths and the discipline which attaches to them).

In their turn covetousness, wickedness, indolence, pride,
and doubt nourish and perpetuate *ignorance*.

Starting afresh from *ignorance*, we may continue the
chains as follows:

*Ignorance*—understood as wrong knowledge—gives
rise to mental formations (volitions, etc.).

These, being conditioned by wrong knowledge, may
lead to:

Covetousness, wickedness, laziness, indolence, pride,
doubt, and the actions accomplished by the body or
mind, or in speech, which are the expression of these,
will reduce, or prevent the acquisition of:

Attention focused on useful objects—clear consciousness of the impressions we feel—faith in the Doctrine of
the Four Truths, without which one will not take the
trouble to listen to explanations of them, or otherwise
study them. They tend also to produce or to increase
negligence in seeking out and frequenting those who have
arrived at comprehension of the Doctrine of the Four
Truths, and who have attained its goal.

On account of lack of mastery over the senses, because the passions darken the intelligence, because physical and mental laziness, doubt, and initial incredulity impede it, the mind cannot keep itself alert, devoting itself to investigations which engender correct knowledge, ready to study the Doctrine which shows the Cause of Suffering and the means by which one puts an end to it; because these same causes lead one to neglect the society of those who are capable of teaching this doctrine, and who may themselves exemplify the results produced by these means; for these various reasons:

*Ignorance* (wrong knowledge) will be continued or increased.

This *Ignorance* (wrong knowledge) will give rise to mental formations (volitions, etc.) inspired by false ideas . . . and the 'cycle' will continue.

In the table which I have given, in Chapter II, of the fundamental theories of Buddhism, I have indicated the abridged form of this cycle: *ignorance—desire—act*, which is attributed to Nâgârjuna, and is current among educated Tibetans. These—I speak of our contemporaries—seem often to be strongly opposed to the semi-popular theories developed in such works as the *Bardo thöd dol*, which depict the pilgrimage of an entity not unlike the *jîva* of the Hindus or the soul of the Christians, which wanders under the influence of *ignorance*, of *mental formations*, and the other articles of the *pratîtyasamûtpâda*, which then become, in some sort, acts accomplished or experienced by an individual.

Nothing transmigrates, say the opponents of these theories. The thing which now exists did not exist before; it has been produced by a number of causes at the moment when it arose (or was born).

The thread which unites the twelve articles of the *pratîtyasamûtpâda* is pure activity, and one may consider that the existence of the 'group' which is held to be a 'person' ends with each revolution of the cycle of the *pratîtyasamûtpâda*, for the action of this revolution is to produce one, or several, other 'groups'.

The illusion which makes us believe in the prolonged stability of the 'groups' (beings or things) is an effect of the inferiority of our means of physical and mental perception. In reality the 'group' is a vortex in which the *mental formations, consciousness, body and mind*, the *senses, contact, sensation, desire, grasping, becoming, birth*, and *dissolution* (death) move, mingle, and are interwoven. And this 'group-vortex' forms itself, disintegrates, and reforms itself at every moment.

Regarding Tibetan Buddhism, my various informants, again and again, reminded me that none of the 'origins' mentioned in the *pratîtyasamûtpâda* can be regarded as an isolated and independent source of action, and that even *ignorance* ranks only as a co-operating cause. This is shown by the word *rkyén*, repeated in each part of the list instead of *rgyud*, which would be a cause able to operate of itself. But it should be noted that those who profess these theories do not admit that anything can be the work of one single cause, and *rgyud* serves, in their language, merely to indicate a principal cause, with which are always associated secondary or co-operating causes, *rkyén*.

We shall return to this problem of ignorance, and the great importance which is given to it in the Buddhist doctrine, when we consider the fourth of the fundamental 'Truths', the Way which leads to Deliverance from Suffering. It is enough to add, here, that ignorance is regarded, by the Buddhists, as the gravest of faults (a 'stain' is the word used by the Buddhist Scriptures), and the worst of mental defilements.

'Laziness is the ruin of homes, idleness is the ruin of beauty, negligence is the ruin of the watcher.

'Unchastity is a stain on a woman, miserliness is a stain on the donor. To do evil is a stain in this and other worlds.

'But greater than all these stains, ignorance is the worst of all. O Disciples, throw off this stain and be stainless.' (Dhammapada.)

Finally, before closing this chapter, let us recall that *ignorance*, about which revolves the cycle of the *pratîtya-samûtpâda*, is well explained as being ignorance of the 'Four Truths' (Suffering, Cause of Suffering, Destruction of Suffering, the Way which leads to Deliverance from Suffering), but that it is more especially ignorance of the fact that there does not exist in the 'person', nor in anything whatever, a permanent and uncompounded 'ego'.

# V

# THE EIGHTFOLD PATH

THE conditions which produce suffering have been shown to us by the *pratîtyasamûtpâda*, which is the object of the second and third of the 'Four Truths' on which Buddhism is based. The Fourth Truth aims at depicting the 'Way' which leads to Deliverance from Suffering; in other words, the means by which the effect of the 'Interdependent Origins' can be checked and destroyed.

The technical name of this Way to Deliverance is the *Eightfold Path* or the *Path with Eight Branches*. We are shown the eight branches in the concise form of a list of eight items, divided into three parts, relating, respectively, to *wisdom*, *morality*, and *concentration of mind*. As follows:

1. Right Views
2. Right Resolve } Wisdom

3. Right Speech
4. Right Action
5. Right Living
6. Right Effort } Morality

7. Right Attention
8. Right Meditation } Concentration of Mind

In the Pâli, Sanscrit, and Tibetan texts the same adjective qualifies each of the eight items in this list; *Sammâ* in Pâli, *samyak* in Sanscrit, *yang dagpa* in Tibetan; all three expressing the idea of perfection.

The Eightfold Path constitutes the programme of action which Buddhism proposes to its followers in order to combat and destroy Suffering. And as Suffering was shown to us as the work of the 'Twelve Interdependent Origins', we can say that the Eightfold Path and the *pratîtyasamûtpâda* are opposed as two adversaries.

*Ignorance* has been indicated as the cause of suffering; the Path opposes to *Ignorance*, *Right Views*, i.e. knowledge.

Right Views come at the head of the list of the subdivisions of the Path, and are the most important of them. Or, rather, one may say that Right Views govern the whole programme of eight items; that they exist only by virtue of them and for them, each of the other seven items playing only a subsidiary rôle, and collaborating in the formation and maintenance of Right Views.

One's first steps in the system of moral and intellectual training which is the Path, depend on a Right View. This initial Right View is the thought which comes to a man who stops and asks himself: Is it reasonable on my part, is it salutary, to follow, unreflectingly, the sheeplike flock which goes its way, baa-ing in chorus, without knowing why? Have I examined the doctrines which I profess, the opinions which I express? Am I certain that the acts which I accomplish are in sober truth those which it is decent, wise, and useful to perform? I will examine my beliefs and my conduct, and will satisfy myself as to whether they are well-founded or not, whether they lead to happiness or to sorrow. To this resolve is added the determination impartially to examine doctrines and systems other than those that one has followed hitherto, in order to judge of their value.

Naturally Buddhists consider as a Right View that which leads one to turn to the teaching of the Buddha, and to give the theories and the methods which he recommends an honest trial.

Although they are not shown there as a ninth item, it should be understood that Right Views, which head the list of the subdivisions of the Path, also end it, as its achievement, its crown. The object of the Path is, in effect, to lead one to right and perfect knowledge, and so to liberate one from *samsâra* (the illusory and painful 'round'), enabling one to reach what Buddhists call 'the other bank', where another aspect of things is perceived, and where our vain reasonings and speculations, having become objectless, fall away from us.

Like the chain of Interdependent Origins, the Eightfold Path has been the subject of numerous commentaries, and not all Buddhists envisage it in the same manner. With the Theravadins the general tendency is to accentuate its character as a moral code. Nyanâtiloka, representing the attitude of his colleagues, the Buddhist monks of Ceylon, writes:

'Every altruistic and noble undertaking is necessarily based on a certain degree of right understanding (a

Right View), no matter who is responsible for it—a Buddhist, a Hindu, a Christian, a Moslem, or even a materialist. It is for this reason that right understanding (or Right Views) stands at the beginning of the Path as its first subdivision. Nevertheless, the order in which the different "branches" are "perfected" is: Morality, concentration of mind, wisdom.'

'Thus', concluded Nyanâtiloka, 'Right Views are the Alpha and Omega of the whole teaching of the Buddha.'

All Buddhists are agreed as to the opinion expressed in his last phrase, but they are by no means unanimous in accepting the order of perfection as given above.

Here is the order in which I have heard educated lamas classify them:

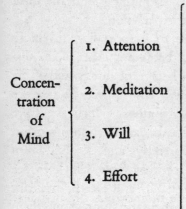

Concen- tration of Mind

1. Attention
2. Meditation
3. Will
4. Effort

The common origin of these four items of the programme of spiritual training named the 'Path' is a first *Right View*, which brings understanding of the usefulness of the search for the Truth. The practice of these four exercises produces, later, *Right Views* of a superior kind, i.e. leads to *Wisdom*.

In the same degree as the *Views* approach perfection— that is to say, where Wisdom increases:

$$\text{Morality} \left\{ \begin{array}{l} \text{5. Speech} \\ \text{6. Action} \\ \text{7. Living} \end{array} \right\} \text{also become more and more perfect.}$$

We will now examine, separately, each of these 'branches' in turn.

## ATTENTION

What do Buddhists mean by *attention*? A verse of the Dhammapada will tell us.

'Vigilance (attentive observation) is the Way which leads to immortality. Negligence is the Way of death. Those who are vigilant do not die. Those who are negligent are already as though they were dead.'

These incisive statements, astonishing both in form and in their content, call for explanation.

Vigilance, attention, leads to immortality, or, more accurately, to Deathlessness,[1] because it leads to the discovery of the real nature of beings, of things, and of the world, which we see under a false aspect, because we regard them through false notions, which we have adopted without any critical examination. Vigilant attention leads us to see correctly, and, so Buddhism tells us, to attain to a point of view from which we see beyond the pairs of opposites: Life and Death, existence and non-existence, as our fragmentary vision shows them to us.

---

[1] The meaning generally given to immortality is: not to die after being born. The idea of Deathlessness, as it is understood by Buddhists, includes that of 'not being born' and corresponds more to our idea of eternity.

He who does not practice attention is the plaything of the multiple influences with which he comes into contact; he is like a drifting cork which is at the mercy of the waves. He does not react; he unconsciously submits to the action of his physical and psychical environment. He is a corpse.

In a general way, attention consists in being first of all attentive to all one's movements and one's acts, both physical and mental. Nothing of what goes on in us should escape us. Neither should we miss anything which happens around us, within the range of our senses.

The Buddhist Scriptures tell us, that one must be conscious that one gets up when one gets up, that one sits down when one sits down, and so on, with all movements.

We should be conscious of the feelings which arise in us, and recognize them: Now there is born in me covetousness, or anger; now sensual desires are arising. Or: I have just had a noble thought, a generous impulse, etc. Or again: I feel depressed, or excited; I am overcome by lassitude; nothing interests me; I am interested only in trivial things. Or: I feel that I am full of energy, I am eager to study, anxious to work for the good of others, etc. . . .

When the power of attention is enhanced, and one has reached the point where one misses none of the phenomena which are occurring in and around oneself, one proceeds to investigate them, and to search for their causes.

Why should anger suddenly blaze up in me? Because

this man has offended me, has injured me. Have I, or
have I not, given expression to sentiments which have
caused him to offend me, to injure me? Is it, on his
part, a deserved vengeance? Has he acted from stupidity,
blindly, led by wrong views as to what is profitable to
him in one way or another?

And what effect will my impulse of anger produce
in me? Will it in any way profit me? Am I going to
show it in my acts? What acts does it suggest that I
should perform? What might be the results of these
acts?—The examination is continued in this way, multi-
plying questions, inquiring if the anger is well-founded,
reasonable, profitable.

All the feelings—envy, sensuality, etc.—may be the
objects of this kind of examination. One must associate
with them the more refined feelings of pride, vanity,
etc. . . . and also those feelings which are considered
praiseworthy: sympathy, benevolence, modesty, etc.

He who practises attention, according to the Buddhist
methods, should not give way to his impulses without
examining them. Neither should he approve or blame
himself, basing his blame or approval on the injunctions
of moral codes whose authority and justness he has not
investigated.

If he performs a charitable deed, if he accomplishes
an act of devotion, he should question himself as to the
motives which he obeyed, should scrutinize his feelings
and their origins, just as when he has committed an
action said to be evil. The result of this kind of inter-

rogation will often result in a shifting of moral values, and will show in a much less favourable light the noble action on which one was ready to pride oneself.

The attention which one directs upon oneself must also be brought to bear on one's surroundings, both people and things. They should be scrutinized, without ill will, calmly and impartially. The first revelation which attention brings to us is that both we and others are poor things, very much to be pitied; and this discovery once made, the Buddhist views all creatures and himself with profound compassion.

To sum up, the practice of perfect attention is a means of learning to know oneself, to know the world in which one lives, and consequently to acquire *Right Views*.

Buddhists have devised numerous exercises for the systematic cultivation of the faculty of attention, which give the senses and the mind a special acuteness of perception.

Faithful to their conception of the 'Chain of Interdependent Origins', which regards this as applying especially to man, the Hinayânists concentrate their *attention* especially on man. They distinguish four 'Fundamental Attentions', as follows:

1. Observation of the body.
2. Observation of the sensations.
3. Observation of the thoughts.
4. Observation of the internal phenomena and workings of the mind.

1. Observation of the body includes:

(a) Observation of the breathing.

'With attentive mind, the disciple breathes in and breathes out. When he makes a long inhalation he knows: I make a long inhalation. When he makes a long exhalation, he knows: I make a long exhalation.

'Similarly the disciple perceives, being fully conscious of it, when the inhalation and exhalation are short. He trains himself in calming the respiratory function, in controlling it, saying to himself: I am going to inhale, I am going to exhale, slowly or quickly.'

He then observes his body, and the bodies of others; he observes the appearance and disappearance of bodies; he understands: Bodies alone are present here.

(b) Observation of the positions of the body:

'The disciple is fully conscious of his position, whether he is walking, sitting, standing, or lying. He understands, according to the circumstances: I am walking, I am sitting, I am standing, or, I am lying.'

He observes himself thus, he observes others, and he understands: There are only bodies present here.

How should we understand these enigmatical statements: He understands *according to the truth*: I am walking, etc. . . . or: He understands: There are only bodies present here? Here is what we are told by an orthodox commentary current among Buddhist believers of the Hinyâna Sect:

'When he says: *I* am walking, *I* am sitting, *I* am standing, *I* am lying, the understanding disciple grasps that there is no permanent person, no real "ego" who walks, sits, stands, or lies. He understands that it is simply by a convention of speech that one attributes these acts to an "I" which has no existence.'

The same lesson is implicit in the statement: *There are only bodies present here*. The disciple should understand that only transitory forms are in question, that there is nothing there save passing appearance, but no man, no woman, nor any real and lasting 'ego'.

(*c*) Observation of his movements.

'The disciple is fully conscious when he goes, when he comes, when he looks at an object, when he turns aside his eyes from it. He is fully conscious when he bends himself, or when he straightens himself, fully conscious in eating, in drinking, in tasting, in satisfying his natural needs, in falling asleep, in waking, in speaking, and in remaining silent.'

The commentary explains to us that in performing these various actions the disciple is conscious of his *intention:* of his *advantage*, of his *duty*, and of the *reality*.

This last word brings him back to the recognition of the unreality of the permanent 'ego' in whose existence the dupes of illusion believe.

(*d*) Observation of the impurity of the body.

The disciple submits his body to a kind of anatomical survey: he 'considers it under the aspect of a bag (the skin) filled with unclean things: bone, marrow, blood, bile; and various organs: heart, lungs, liver, stomach, entrails.' The description does not spare us any unpleasant detail: it includes the secretions, mucus, excrement.

(e) Analysis of the body.

'The disciple concludes that the body, which goes and comes, which performs various actions, is nothing but a product of the combinations of the four elementary forces: solidity, fluidity, heat, movement; which may also be regarded as: inertia, cohesion, radiation, and vibration (the four elementary forces usually symbolized as the four elements, earth, water, fire, wind).

(f) Meditations on mortality.

These meditations took place, formerly, in the actual cemeteries; those cemeteries of ancient India into which corpses were thrown without burial, and where they awaited, for days on end, their cremation, when they were cremated. The macabre spectacle which these meditations demand is less easy to find in our days, although the sight of corpses is by no means rare in India or in Tibet. However, the Hinayânist monks often content themselves with pictures reproducing the nine scenes described in the texts, or, more simply still, merely picture them in imagination.

Here are the nine pictures according to the *Digha-Nikâya*:

(1) A corpse which has lain in the cemetery for one, two, or three days, swollen, blue-black, rotting.

(2) A corpse lying in the cemetery, torn by crows and vultures, the flesh eaten by jackals and riddled by worms.

(3) A bloody skeleton with a few shreds of flesh attached.

(4) A fleshless skeleton, stained with blood, held together by the sinews.

(5) A skeleton with no flesh, no sign of blood, held together by the sinews.

(6) Scattered bones. Here a bone from the hand, there a bone from the foot; here a bit of the spinal column; farther away, the skull.

(7) The same bones whitened by time, turned the colour of shells.

(8) These bones piled in a heap, a year later.

(9) These bones desiccated and reduced to dust.

And after each of these contemplations, the disciple tells himself: 'Even so will my body become; even so the bodies of others. He considers how bodies arise, how they disappear. He tells himself: There is nothing but bodies there (and no permanent "ego"). Then he possesses understanding, penetration; he lives independently, free from attachment to anything in the world.'

'He who has practised this attention applied to the body will overcome all tendency to discontent; he will not be dominated by fear or by anxiety. He will endure, with calmness, heat, cold, hunger, thirst, bad weather, angry or insulting words, and physical suffering.'

II. *Observation of the Sensations.*

The disciple observes the pleasant sensations and the unpleasant sensations which he experiences. He observes those shown by others, and he tells himself: There is nothing here but sensations (meaning that there is no permanent 'ego' here).

III. *Observation of the thoughts.*

The disciple, as fast as his thoughts arise, notes their nature: Thoughts of envy, of anger; thoughts caused by error, and thoughts free from error. He perceives that his thoughts are concentrated, or, on the contrary, that they are dispersed. He perceives his noble and elevated thoughts, and those which are vile and debased. He perceives his lasting thoughts and his fugitive thoughts, his free thoughts and those which are suggested to him and imposed on him.

He observes also what he can perceive of the thoughts of others, and says to himself: There is nothing there but thoughts (meaning that there is no permanent 'ego' there).

IV. *Observation of internal phenomena and the workings of the mind.*

(1) The disciple perceives when there is sensuality in him, or anger, or restfulness, or excitement, or agitation, or doubt. He also knows when he is free from them. He knows how sensuality, anger, restfulness, etc., are produced, and he knows how to master them.

(2) The disciple observes the five elements (*skandhas*) which make up what we call a 'person'; that is to say: physical form—sensation—perception—the mental creations—consciousness. He observes how each of these

constituent elements of the group called 'person' arises and then disappears.

(3) The disciple knows how ties are formed as the result of the senses and their objects (by the effect of contact and the resulting sensation), and he knows how one can break these ties.

(4) The disciple discerns when attention, the search for truth, interest, calm, concentration, serenity, exist in himself, and when he is devoid of them. He discerns: Such and such of these qualities are not in me. He knows how the elements of knowledge come into being and how they are brought to perfection.

Another practice included in the Buddhist system of the cultivation of attention consists in exercising the memory as follows: At the end of the day one recalls the actions which one has performed, the feelings which one has experienced, the thoughts which one has entertained. The examination is conducted *backwards*; that is to say, beginning with the last sensation one has felt, the last action performed, the last thought one has entertained, and working back until the first moments after waking.

The most insignificant things should be recalled equally with the most important, for which it is good to estimate, in passing, the value of the various internal or external vicissitudes through which one has passed. The aim of the exercise is simply to teach us to allow none of the things which our senses have perceived, or the ideas which have passed through our minds, to become obliterated.

Buddhism assigns to the memory[1] a rôle of the greatest importance. One of its precepts is that nothing must be forgotten. Everything that one has seen, heard, or perceived, no matter how, even only once and only for a minute, should be registered in the memory and never effaced.

The constant presence of mind, the firm will, and the ever-active clairvoyance recommended by Buddhism depend largely upon the possibility of an instantaneous, and, as it were, automatic appeal to the innumerable experiments and analyses of all kinds which have been previously carried out.

The examination of a single day is only an exercise for a beginner. After a period of training, the duration of which varies according to the abilities of those who undergo it, the examination embraces, in succession, two days, a week, a month; sometimes including not only the incidents noted during the waking state, but also the dreams which have followed one another during sleep. Certain general recapitulations of the bygone phases of life may include several years, and go back as far as the early days of childhood.

This exercise is not peculiar to Buddhism; it is known to most of the Hindu schools of mental training, and is strongly recommended by them.

Among the innumerable sensations which have affected

---

[1] Memory (as enjoined upon the disciple) consists in never forgetting the beings or things with which one has been in contact (Ashidharma of the Tibetans).

his organism, only a minute proportion show themselves in conscious and coordinated fashion in the memory of the individual; the others remain inert, or manifest themselves only by confused impulses and tendencies. What we call heredity and atavism can be assimilated, in this sense, to the remote memory of elements which are present in our existing person. Thus, there are those who believe that patient training may act like the developer which, applied to an exposed photographic plate, brings out the images which were impressed upon it, but which remained invisible.

We can without difficulty accept the idea of bringing to light some part of the content of our subconscious, or even its entire content, but many will find it difficult to believe in the possibility of reviving, in our present consciousness, the memory of sensations which impressed certain of the elements which compose our present person when they formed a part of other 'groups', individuals, or things.

However impracticable this search for eternal life in the past may seem to us, it is by no means irrational in principle. The Westerners who have argued so much about the nature of the next world, and the mystery of the after-life, are hardly justified in deriding those who pursue the mystery of the 'before-birth,' for this, after all, does not exceed the limits of reality, and consists in data which have actually occurred, in matter which *has existed*, and which consequently may and even must have left traces.

At the same time, it should be remembered that in Buddhism no theories rank as dogmas, and those which have just been expounded are by no means part of a stock of essential doctrines propounded by the canonical books.

The developments of the precept concerning *Perfect Attention* lead us to psycho-analysis, which has only recently been taken seriously in the West, but which has been practised for centuries among Buddhists. We have already seen that the disciple is enjoined to be conscious of all inner happenings due to his mental activity, and to seek the proximate causes of these happenings, so as to estimate their value, and that of the corresponding reaction; as in the example which I gave of the man who became angry because he considered himself offended by another man. As he progresses in the exercise of attention the disciple is expected to carry his investigations below this 'surface' of his consciousness.

The offence which he has suffered is only the 'occasion' which allowed one of his propensities to show itself. Whence comes this propensity? What, in the composition of his physical body or his mentality, is the origin of this propensity: what keeps it alive, nourishes it? The research is almost always arduous, the more so because Buddhists conceive the 'person' as an unstable group, so that such and such an element, which entered into its composition yesterday, and by its presence caused a propensity to anger, may today have been eliminated, or may well have sunk back into the unfathomable obscurity of the secret depths of the 'person'. Besides the 'occasion', which, in the case under investigation, is an offence, and the 'propensity' to anger, other factors are at work. The 'propensity' to anger does not arise suddenly from nothing. It is surrounded by other propensities which influence it, which strengthen or restrain it, and the 'occasion' also is modified by subsidiary circumstances of place, environment, time, etc., which increase or diminish its power and the influence which it exerts on the 'propensity'.

A very minute and profound research into the realm of the subconscious (which the Tibetan mystics usually call 'the depths of the mind') is carried out by the disciples of some Tibetan masters. And here one peculiarity must be noted. While in the West hypnotic methods often play a part in such investigations of the subconscious, so that the investigator is dealing with a subject whose will has previously been more or less paralysed, in Tibet the disciple is taught and trained with a view to making this investigation in respect of his own person, and without the cooperation of any alien personality.

We must note also that this training aims at the attainment of a reality which far surpasses the simple truth as it appears to the man whose inner vision is insufficiently developed.

It has recently been announced that an American scientist has discovered a potion which compels those who drink it to tell the truth: that is to say, the superficial truth as it appears to the subject, but which may no longer be the truth when one probes beneath the surface.

The inquiry which is allied with *Right Attention* does go beneath the surface.

Another application of *Right Attention* is attention to dreams.

Like the Hindu Vedantists, many Buddhists consider the habitual absence of dreams as a sign of mental perfection. Those who have not attained to it are advised to force themselves to remain conscious while dreaming: in other words, to *know* that they are dreaming.

Western philosophers and doctors have declared that such a thing is impossible. When one knows that one is dreaming, they say, one is already almost awake. It is difficult for Westerners who have not lived for many years among the Asiatics of India, China, or Tibet, and who have not had long practical experience of their methods, to understand the psychic possibilities of these peoples, trained for centuries in an utterly different direction to that in which the religions of Semitic origin have led us.

To be conscious that one is dreaming, while the dream unfolds itself, and one experiences the appropriate sensations, seems in no way extraordinary in the East. Some men even apply themselves, without waking, to reflections upon the data which their dream presents to them. Sometimes they contemplate, with the interest one takes in a theatrical performance, the succession of adventures which they live through in their sleep. I have heard some say that they have sometimes hesitated to commit, in dreams, actions which they would not have wished to perform when awake, and that being moved by the desire to experience the sensation which their action would procure for them, they have put aside their scruples, because they knew that the action which they were about to commit was not real, and would have no repercussions on the life which they would recommence on awaking.—Would it have none in reality? Opinions on this subject are divided.

Tsong Khapa, the reformer of Tibetan Buddhism, and the founder of the Gelugspa Sect,[1] which today constitutes the official clergy of Tibet, considers it most important to keep control of oneself during sleep.

In his principal work, the *Lam-rim*, he states: It is essential not to waste the time given to sleep, either by remaining, when once asleep, inert as a stone, or by allowing one's mind to wander incoherently in absurd or harmful dreams. The disorderly manifestations of mental activity to which he submits in dreams cost the sleeper an expenditure of energy which could have been applied to some useful purpose. Moreover, the action performed or the thoughts experienced while dreaming have results identical with those of the actions and thoughts of the man when awake. So it is needful, wrote Tsong Khapa, not to 'manufacture evil' while asleep.

---

[1] *Gelugspa* = 'those who have virtuous customs'. Generally called 'Yellow Hats,' as the reformer ordered them to wear this head-dress so as to distinguish them from the monks who had not accepted his reform, and who wore red hats.

This theory will probably astonish many Westerners. How, they will ask, can an imaginary deed have the same results as a real action? Should we then imprison the man who has dreamt that he stole the purse of some passer-by?

This is an irrelevant comparison, for it does not correspond with the standpoint of Tsong Khapa and many other Buddhists. For them, there can be no question of 'prison', nor of a 'judge' condemning the robber. They do not believe in the retribution of good and evil by a conscious and personal power. In the people's eyes the rôle of *Yama*, Judge of the Dead, consists merely in applying inflexible laws of which he is not the author, and which he has no power to change in any way. Also, when they teach the practice of *Attention* continued through the period of sleep, Tsong Khapa and the other Buddhist masters who share his views are not speaking to the common herd, but only to those who are already familiar with the doctrines relating to the constitution of the 'group' which we, quite wrongly, take as the 'ego'. According to them, the most serious consequences of thoughts or actions are not those which are visible and external, but the modifications of a psychic order which they produce in the individual responsible for them. The will to accomplish an act, even if it is not afterwards consummated, creates, in him who has had the will or the desire, affinities and tendencies which bring about a change in his character.

This assiduous watch over one's conduct while dreaming brings us back to the investigation of the subconscious, to psycho-analysis.

In the course of our development, says Freud, we have effected a division of our mental life; we have divided it into a coherent 'ego' and an unconscious and repressed portion, which is left outside the former. In dreams, that which is thus excluded knocks, seeking to enter the gates, although these are guarded by resistances.

Freud was not the first to perceive this intrusion of the contents of the subconscious into the consciousness of the sleeper, and its consequences; the peculiar dreams in which the sleeper feels sentiments which are in no way habitual with him, thinks and acts in an unaccustomed fashion, and in short, assumes a personality other than that which is his when awake.

Tsong Khapa, in the fifteenth century, basing his opinion, we are told, on an older teaching, believed that the manifestations of our real nature are fettered by the state of constraint which is always ours in our waking state, when we are conscious of our social personality, our surroundings, the teachings and examples which are always present in our memory, and a thousand other things. The secret of this real nature resides in the impulses which are in no way governed by such considerations. Sleep, in abolishing these limiting factors, to a great extent liberates the mind from the fetters by which it is bound in the waking state, and gives freer play to the natural impulses.

According to this theory it is therefore the real individual who acts in dreams, and his acts, even though they are imaginary from the standpoint of one who is awake, are very real as volitions, and involve all the consequences attached to the latter; that is to say, as we have already seen, they modify the character of the individual.

Many masters of the Mahâyâna, basing themselves on these ideas, recommend a careful watch over one's conduct during dreams, and over the sentiments which one experiences while dreaming, in order to learn to know oneself. They nevertheless advise their disciples to apply themselves to discerning the effects upon the sleeper's consciousness of memories derived from the waking state, or of physical sensations. For example, a man who is cold while sleeping may dream that he is camping in the snow with some companions. But if in the course of his dream he takes away the blanket or the coat covering one of his comrades, in order to get warm by wrapping himself in it, this imaginary act shows a real tendency to egoism in the sleeper. If, in his dream, the sleeper uses violence in order to appropriate his comrade's blanket, one may conclude that his egoism and his desire for comfort outweigh his feelings of benevolence and humanity, and might, should the occasion offer itself, lead him to acts of violence while awake.

Some of the exercises which the Hinayânists include in their programme for training the *Attention* are criticized, and even entirely disapproved of by other Buddhists.

Among these exercises is the *Contemplation of the Impurity of the Body* described above. 'It is as absurd to despise the body as to admire it', a Chinese monk said to me. To consider certain things repulsive, to feel disgust for them, and, what is worse, to cultivate this disgust, is contrary to Buddhist teaching, which condemns such distinctions.

And further, the *Meditations on Mortality* practised as already described are likewise regarded as valueless by many Mahâyânists, who condemn them as attaching an unmerited importance to the physical body, and wrongly connecting its dissolution with the dissolution of our personality. Why, they ask, lay oneself out to provoke emotion at the disintegration of a human body? This disintegration is of the same kind as that of a plant or stone. The enlightened Buddhist sees the law of impermanency at work in all things, and regards their dissolution with equal serenity.

Among the Mahâyânists, the exercise of *Attention* often aims at impressing on the mind the spectacle of the mobility of mental formations.

The disciple is recommended to seat himself in an isolated spot, and there, in tranquillity, to contemplate the procession of thoughts and subjective images which, without his having willed or desired them, arise within him spontaneously, hurrying and jostling like the waves of a torrent. The disciple should attentively consider this rapid procession, without attempting to stop its flow. Thus he gradually comes to understand that the world resembles this procession which he watches in himself, that it consists in a succession of phenomena arising and disappearing with dizzy rapidity. He *sees* that, as the Buddhist philosopher Santarakshita[1] (eighth century) taught, 'The essence of reality is movement.'

The origin of this movement is unknowable. It is 'energy arising by itself', as the Buddhist writers of Tibet say. The disciple, then, is not expected to seek for the initial cause which engendered this energy, for that would be merely to refer the problem back, since he would then have to inquire what had produced this cause, and proceeding thus from cause to cause, to pursue his research eternally. That which he ought to *see* is life as it manifests itself in the space of one moment.

The assiduous practice of attention by this method is said to lead one to perceive surrounding objects, and also oneself, in the form of a vortex of moving elements. A tree, a stone, an animal, cease to be seen as solid bodies, enduring for a relatively long period of time, and in their place the trained disciple discerns a continual succession of sudden manifestations, lasting only the time of a lightning-flash, the apparent continuity of the objects which he watches, and of his own person, being caused by the rapidity with which these 'flashes' follow one another.

The disciple, having reached this stage, has attained

[1] Santarakshita, an Indian from Gaur, abbot of the great monastery of Nalanda, introduced Buddhism into Tibet.

to what Buddhists mean by *Right Views*. He has *seen* that phenomena are due to the perpetual operations of energies, without having as a basis any substance from which they emerge; he has *seen* that impermanence is the universal law, and that the 'ego' is a pure illusion due to a lack of insight and a deficient power of perception.

It may be of interest, at this point, to give an idea of the way in which the Tibetans apply themselves to the observation of the mind. The extracts below are translated from the *Phyag chen gyi zin bris* (pronounced *Chag chen gyi zindi*).

'(1) The mind should be observed in its tranquil state of repose.

'(2) One must examine the nature of this immobile "thing".

'(3) One must inquire *how* that which we call mind remains quiescent, and how it sets itself in motion by emerging from its tranquillity.'

One must inquire:

'(1) Whether its motion comes from outside the state of tranquillity.

'(2) Whether it moves even when it is at rest.

'(3) Whether its motion is, or is not, another thing than immobility (the state of repose).

'One must inquire what is the order of reality of this movement, and then, what conditions lead to its arrest.'

It is said that after prolonged observation one forms

the opinion that *that* which moves does not differ from *that* which remains immobile.

'This point being reached, one should ask oneself whether the mind which observes *that* which moves and *that* which remains immobile is different from them, whether it is the "ego" of that which moves and of that which remains immobile.

'One sees, then, that the observer and the object observed are inseparable. And as it is impossible to classify these two realities—the observer and the object observed—as being either a duality or unity, they are called: "the goal beyond the mind" and "the goal beyond all theories".'

In the Sutra entitled *The Questions of Kasyapa* it is said:

'By the friction of two sticks, one against the other, fire is produced.

'And by the fire engendered by them, both are consumed.

'So, by the intelligence born of them,

'The couple formed by "the immobile" and the "moving", and the observer, considering their duality, are in the same way consumed.'

Here are some other subjects for investigation suggested in the above-named work.

'Is the mind composed of matter?

'If it is material, of what kind of matter is it composed?

'If it is an objective thing, what is its form and its colour?

'If it is a "knowing" principle, is it an idea which manifests itself temporarily?

'What then is this *immaterial* thing which manifests itself in various *forms*?

'What produces it?

'If the mind were a real entity, it would be possible to consider it as a kind of substance.'

Continuing in this way, the disciple reaches the conclusion that the mind is neither material nor immaterial, and that it cannot be classified in the category of things of which one can say: they *are* or they *are not*.

The disciple also asks himself:

'Is the mind a simple thing?

'Is it a composite thing?

'If it is simple, how does it manifest itself in different ways?

'If it is composite, how can it be brought to this state of "voidness" in which there is nothing but unity?'

Still continuing his investigations, the disciple comes to recognize that the mind is exempt from the two extremes: *unity* and *plurality*.

It is said:

'Before me, behind me, in the ten directions[1]

'Wherever I look I see "Thatness" (identity)[2]

'Today, O my master, illusion is dissipated;

'From now on, I will put no more questions to anyone.'

[1] The four cardinal points, the intercardinal points, the zenith, and the nadir.
[2] Tathâaâ, a Sanscrit term much used in Mahâyâna Buddhism. It means 'the state of being that' = identity. In Tibetan: *tejingni*, written *de bjin nid*: 'the very same', or 'the very that'.

Nagarjuna, the most famous of the Mahâyânist philosophers, is said to have recommended the practice of attention in the following terms:

'Remember that attention has been declared to be the only road followed by the Buddhas. Continually observe thy body (the actions accomplished by the body, the activity of the five senses, their causes, their results), so as to know it.

'Negligence in this observation renders all spiritual exercises vain.

'It is this continual attention which is called "not being distracted".'

And, to conclude this brief study of Buddhist attention, let us recall the definition of the memory, as it is enjoined upon the disciple:

'Memory consists in never forgetting the beings and the things with which one has been in contact, even if only on one occasion.' (Abhidharma.)

## MEDITATION

Buddhists are unanimous in defining Right Meditation as being the concentration of thought upon a single object. But apart from this initial definition there is no unanimity. Buddhists have invented innumerable practices to which they give the name of 'meditation'. In spite of their number it is not impossible to classify them, and, in a general way, we can divide them into two categories.

(1) Practices which are intended to act on the mind,

to implant in it tendencies which did not previously exist, to strengthen certain tendencies already existing, or to eliminate others among them.

In the same category can be placed those practices tending to produce states of consciousness other than that which is habitual with us, so as to perceive, by this means, facts or objects which cannot be known to us in our ordinary state of consciousness. It can also be said that these practices aim at inducing intuition.

On a lower plane, also, we can include in this category exercises designed to produce peace of mind and serenity, indispensable preludes to vigilance, analysis, and investigation, and all that is included in *Right Attention*.

(2) Exercises whose aim is to calm and then arrest the agitation of the mind, to curb the activity of the wandering imagination and the production of spontaneous ideas which arise uninvited, and then disappear in the mind, continually replaced by new ideas. Exercises of this kind tend to discipline thought and to compel it to direct itself upon the object presented to it, and to remain fixed upon that object without wandering from it. Another of their aims is the complete suppression of all thoughts belonging to our ordinary state of consciousness, in order to uncover the depths of the mind which these thoughts conceal from us.

In Western phraseology, we should say that the objective pursued is to make contact with the subconscious.

This suppression of mental activity is mentioned by

the ancient masters of Hindu Yoga. Patanjali defined
meditation as the 'suppression of the movements or
operations of the mind' (*citta vritti nirodha*) and we
find in the commentary of the *Lamdön*[1] the following
definition: 'Meditation is the secret source of the power
to abandon ratiocinations simultaneously with their
seed.'

One must not misunderstand the sense of these statements. Their real meaning is very imperfectly given,
sometimes even completely distorted. In translation,
Patanjali has been represented as saying that meditation
was the 'suppression of the thinking principle'. There
is no question of that. There is no question of interfering
with the intelligence of the individual, of expecting
him to remain inert 'without thinking', although certain
so-called 'spiritual masters' have ordered their disciples
to practise this impossible exercise. The suppression
which is enjoined is, as has already been said, that of
the operations (*vritti*) of the mind which fabricate the
ideas, the suppression of the fantasies of the imagination.
The precept repeated *ad nauseam* in the *Prajñâ Pâramitâ*
and in all philosophic works belonging to this school
is: 'Do not imagine.'

Now let us consider a few exercises belonging to the
first of the above-mentioned categories. We read in the
*Majjhima Nikâya*:

'The disciple lives a holy life, a virtuous life, he is

[1] Written: Lam sgron, *The Lamp of the Way*. A Tibetan work.

master of his senses, and clearly conscious. He seeks a lonely place where he can establish himself, either in the forest, at the foot of a tree, or in a cave on a mountain.

'At midday, when the disciple has finished eating the food which he has begged, he seats himself cross-legged, his body upright, his mind alert and concentrated.

'He rejects covetousness, his thoughts are freed from covetousness, his heart is liberated from covetousness.

'He rejects anger, his thoughts are freed from anger. Entertaining loving thoughts toward all living beings, he liberates his heart from anger.

'He rejects indifference. Loving the light, with vigilant mind, with clairvoyant consciousness, he frees his heart from indifference.

'He rejects agitation, the wandering of the mind, his heart remains peaceful; he frees his mind from agitation.

'He rejects doubt. Full of confidence in Wisdom, he frees his mind from doubt.

'He has rejected the five obstacles and learnt to know the fetters which paralyse the mind.

'And now, having purified his mind, the disciple can begin the four Lower *Jhânas*.'

The Pali word *Jhâna* is equivalent to the Sanskrit *Dhyana*, and has been preferred here because it is especially the Hinâyâna Scriptures, written in Pali, which discuss the *Jhânas*. *Jhâna* is generally translated by 'ecstasy' or by 'trance', but I suggest 'states of consciousness' as an approximate translation. It is far from perfect, but 'ecstasy', which recalls the transports of mystics in communion with the object of their worship, and, still more, 'trance', which makes one think of the mediums in spiritualistic séances, are both wholly inadequate. In any case, the reader can see for himself what the *Jhânas* are from the following description:

(1) Having rejected those impressions which lead the senses astray, having rejected evil things, the disciple, reasoning and reflecting, enters into the *First Jhâna*, a state of enthusiasm and joy born of concentration.

The *First Jhâna* is free from covetousness, anger, indifference, agitation of mind, and doubt. There are present in it reasoning, reflection, enthusiasm, and joy.

(2) Having suppressed reasoning and reflection, but retaining enthusiasm and joy, the disciple obtains that inner peace and single-mindedness which constitute the *Second Jhâna*.

(3) After enthusiasm has evaporated, the disciple remains serene, his senses and perceptions alert, his consciousness clairvoyant. Then he experiences in his heart the feeling of which the Sages say: 'Happy is the man who possesses serenity and a reflective mind.' He thus enters the *Third Jhâna*.

(4) Finally, when the disciple has rejected pleasure and suffering, when he has renounced past joy and sorrow, he enters into the state of serenity, liberated from pleasure and suffering, into the neutral state of clairvoyance of mind which is the *Fourth Jhâna*.

These four *Jhânas*, by a gradual progress, thus lead the

disciple to mental attitudes more and more closely approximating to the perfect attitude as Buddhism conceives it. Beyond these four *Jhânas*, which I have called the lower, Buddhists speak of four others of quite a different character. We will study them in their turn.

Let us now consider a kind of meditation included in our first category, which aims at arousing certain sentiments in him who practises it.

A classical example of these meditations exists: that of the 'Four Infinite Sentiments' or the 'Four Sublime Sentiments'. It is described in the *Mahâ-Sudassana Sutta*, a work presenting certain analogies with the literary form of the Apocalypse. The Buddha relates to his cousin and disciple Ananda the events which form the subject of the book. Facts and personages are imaginary, and the action takes place in a world of phantasy. Here is the passage which concerns the meditation of the hero: the Great and Glorious King.

'The Great and Glorious King, O Ananda, mounted to the Chamber of the Great Collection.'[1] (This picturesque expression is sometimes thought to mean that the hero has retired into himself, the 'collection' being understood as the elements which constitute the 'person'. Others regard the 'Great Collection' as being the three worlds—of desire, of form, and formless—with all the beings therein. There are many other interpre-

[1] Or 'assembly', or 'group'.

tations.) And halting on the threshold, he cried with
intense emotion:

'Back! Come no farther, O thoughts of envy. Back!
Come no farther, thoughts of covetousness! Back!
Come no farther, thoughts of hatred!'

Then he entered into the chamber and seated himself
on a golden throne. And then, having rejected all
passions, all unrighteous thoughts, he attained the *First
Jhâna*, a state of well-being and of joy, produced by
solitude, a state of reflection and research.

Putting aside reflection and research, he attained the
*Second Jhâna*, a state of joy and well-being produced by
serenity, a state in which reflection and research are
absent, a state of quietude and spiritual elevation.

Ceasing to find pleasure in joy, he remained conscious,
master of himself, and attained the *Third Jhâna*, experi-
encing that intimate comfort which the Sages proclaim,
saying 'He who, master of himself, remains indifferent,
experiences a profound well-being.'

Putting aside this well-being, rejecting sorrow, being
dead to joy as to suffering, he attains that state of the
purest mastery of himself, and of serenity, which is the
*Fourth Jhâna*.

These are, with slight differences of expression, the
four attitudes of mind which have already been described
to us. They are classic in all the sects of Buddhism. But
the spiritual exercise does not stop there. The *Mahâ-
Sudassana Sutta* is inspired by the Mahâyâna, and represents the Glorious King as being the Buddha himself

in one of his former lives; and in order to be faithful to the spirit of the Mahâyâna, the hero will not remain absorbed in himself; he is going to emerge from the 'chamber' and interest himself in the world.

'The Great and Glorious King, O Ananda, then came out from the Chamber of the Great Collection, and entering into the Golden Chamber he seated himself upon a silver throne.

'With loving thought he considered the world, and his love extended itself, in turn, to each of the four regions. Then, his heart full of love, with a love increasing incessantly and immeasurably, he enveloped the whole world to its farthest limits.

'With thoughts of sympathetic pity he considered the world, and his sympathetic pity extended itself, in turn, to each of the four regions. Then, his heart full of sympathetic pity, with this sympathetic pity increasing incessantly and immeasurably, he enveloped the whole world to its farthest limits.

'With thoughts of joy he considered the world, and his joy extended itself, in turn, to each of the four regions. Then, his heart full of joy, with joy increasing incessantly and immeasurably, he enveloped the whole world to its farthest limits.

'With thoughts of serenity he considered the world, and his serenity extended itself, in turn, to each of the four regions. Then, his heart full of serenity, with serenity increasing incessantly and immeasurably, he enveloped the whole vast world to its farthest limits.'

All Buddhists are expected to practise these meditations, following the example of the Great and Glorious King. Their utility and their results are regarded in different ways.

Some think—and not without reason—that he who day by day trains himself to excite in himself certain tendencies, certain sentiments, will in the end make them habitual. This method of developing them, however, meets with objection on the part of those who believe in the purely intellectual training which one is justified in regarding as that which is most in conformity with the original spirit of Buddhism.

They do not deny that the conduct and sentiments of a man may be modified by practices of this kind, but they see in such modification an effect of what we know as auto-suggestion. Practices of this kind are harmful, they say, because they create automatic habits instead of leading to conscious and reasoned actions. Moreover, he who is accustomed to obey suggestions of this kind is liable to fall, at another time, under the influence of suggestions of the opposite order, and to consider the world with hatred, just as he had considered it with love, his hatred being as baseless as was his love.

Another objection relates to the emotional character of the meditation of the 'Four Infinite Sentiments' when it is practised without the accompaniment of reasoning. The disciple who puts himself temporarily into states of mind which are not natural to him is apt to conceive a false opinion of himself, and to believe that he has

actually acquired certain sentiments, although these will
be fictive, and will never be translated into action. In any
case, for that matter, emotion is banned by Buddhism
as akin to intoxication, and contrary to the sober mental
equilibrium which is indispensable for the attainment
of *Right Views*.

The meditation of the 'Infinite Sentiments' is also
envisaged from a purely altruistic point of view. It is
then no longer a question of cultivating the 'Infinite
Sentiments' so as to make them one's own. The effect
sought for is to project upon all beings, by the mental
concentration of the person who is meditating, each
of the 'Four Infinite Sentiments'. To the world which
is suffering because of hatred, or anger, and all the
pernicious sentiments which are manifested in it, the
disciple, in meditation, sends a 'thought-force' which is
love. This should act on the world, influence men's
minds, and incline them to kindliness and friendship.
He sends a thought of sympathetic pity, which will
deaden the pain of those who suffer, of those whom no
one pities. He sends joy, which will increase the joy
of those who are happy and will bring joy to those
who lack it. Finally, he sends thoughts of serenity
which will appease distress and anguish and raging
desires.

Those who conceive the action of the meditation on
the 'Four Infinite Sentiments' in this way hold that
thought is an energy capable of producing effects

whose measure depends on the strength with which it has been emitted.

Again, according to another way of practising the meditation on the 'Four Infinite Sentiments', the disciple begins by fixing his loving thoughts on those who are naturally dearest to him. Then he directs his thoughts toward those who hold a lesser place in his affections, and continuing thus, in descending order, he comes to those who are simply indifferent to him, to whom he wishes no ill, and he transforms the indifference which he feels for them into affection.

Having reached this point, the disciple turns to those who are antipathetic to him, those who are hostile to him; first, to those for whom he feels a slight degree of antipathy, who are slightly hostile to him; people whose opinions or manners irritate him; then, in due order, to people who have offended him slightly, or gravely; to people who have harmed him slightly, or gravely, etc., ending with those whom he regards as his worst enemies, those who inspire in him a mortal hatred—if, of course, he has such enemies.

When he has completed such a survey, mastering his inclinations to ill-will, anger, and hatred, and when he has succeeded—perhaps after repeated efforts, and a long period of time—in considering with sympathy those for whom he felt the strongest aversion, and in wishing them well and being ready to work for their happiness, then he can enlarge the circle of his thoughts and extend them to all parts of the world, those situated to the east of him, to the west, to the south, to the north, respectively, finally embracing the entire universe with all the beings contained in it, human and non-human, in a loving thought.

It should be noted that according to this method the disciple is considered capable of extending an *efficacious* thought of love to the whole world only when his mind and his heart are completely liberated from all feelings of hostility and ill-will; that is to say, when he has succeeded in actually loving those whom he hated or who hated him.

The meditation on the 'Sublime Sentiments', understood in this way, is accompanied by reflection. The disciple should examine the reasons he may have for loving some of those whom he evokes in thought, and he will also examine the reasons he may have for not loving others, or for hating them. Having discovered these reasons, he should weigh their value, and seek also to discover the underlying and distant causes of his sympathies and antipathies. If he replies to the first question which he puts to himself by saying: 'I love this man because he is my father', or perhaps: 'I love this other man because he has done me a service', he should not consider this a final answer. It may happen that after examination he will perceive that between him and his father there exists only a tie formed by habit, that obedience to the suggestion produced by the common opinion of filial love has evoked the sentiment which he thought to be love. It may be that he finds that another man has shown himself more devoted, more generous towards him than the man whom he loves because of some service rendered. Why does he feel affection for the latter, and not for the former?

None of the reasons which we give are final. Beyond them exist causes, and causes of these causes, *ad infinitum*. The 'Infinite Sentiments', to be what they ought to be, energetic, powerful, and active, should be based on solid foundations. A passing rush of emotion must not be taken for one or other of the 'Infinite Sentiments'.

The spiritual masters of Tibet, whose methods are drastic, reverse the order in which the disciple should imagine those toward whom he directs his loving thoughts.

The first to be evoked is he for whom the disciple feels the strongest aversion, or even he who is mortally hated, if such a mortal enemy happens to exist.

We should say, to speak colloquially, that this is to 'seize the bull by the horns', and we can readily believe that when someone has succeeded in convincing himself that he has good reason to love his enemy, he must necessarily embrace in his loving thoughts those toward whom he has not entertained any ill feeling, those to whom he is indifferent, and still more, those who have shown him friendship, who are devoted to him. The Tibetan masters, who are often clever psychologists, state that this is not always the case, and that it is often easier to transmute hatred into love than to awaken love where there is neutral indifference, or even, sometimes, where there is the customary affection felt for relatives.

'Only those sentiments which are founded on reason are durable', the Head Lama of the monastery of Enchay said to me; 'durable, at least, so long as other reflections do not undermine their bases; for nothing in all the world is permanent.' As for love gained by mastering the opposite sentiments which exist in one's mind, by constraining oneself, the same lama declared that such love did not exist. 'If the man who thus does violence to himself procures, by his actions, the well-being of his enemy', said he, 'this means only that he is pretending to love him, but in the depth of his heart there is no real love. After all', the lama added, philosophically, 'this *pretence* is perhaps all that is necessary to enable men to live in peace and to be happy together.' However, this sally was not his last word. 'To have such appearances, even though they contribute to the happiness of others, adds nothing to the spiritual value of a man', he concluded; 'it is our true character which counts, and not the fictitious personality which we superimpose upon it.'

It goes without saying that the three other 'Infinite Sentiments'—sympathetic pity, joy, and serenity—are treated in an analogous fashion in these meditations, and that they give rise to the same differences of opinion and of method.

The Mahâyânist sects, above all those which have

adopted the Tantrik methods, have invented numerous
forms of meditation, which often tend either to lead
the disciple to doubt his own senses, to hold that the
world as shown by the senses is not the reality, or to
bring him to the realization that all that which we
perceive is a projection of our mind.

The programme of spiritual training, among the
Tibetans, is laid down as follows: (1) To regard, to
examine. (2) To reflect, to meditate. (3) To practise.
Or—(1) To seek for the meaning of things, the reason
for things. (2) To study these in detail. (3) To reflect,
to meditate on what has been discovered. (4) To understand.

Perhaps I may be allowed to refer those of my readers
who may be interested in Tibetan methods of spiritual
training to two of my own books: *With Mystics and
Magicians in Tibet*[1] and *Initiations and Initiates in Tibet*.[2]
Although peculiar in form, these methods often tend
toward a goal entirely in conformity with the Buddhist
ideal. I will not enlarge upon them here, for they are
outside the scope of this book.

In Tibet, retirement to a hermitage, or at least, to a
separate room, is considered indispensable for prolonged
periods of meditation. In other Buddhist countries the
monks do not insist so strongly on this point; however,
even if they personally abstain from them, all advocate
periods of retreat devoted to meditation.

[1] John Lane, London. Claude Kendall, New York.
[2] Rivers, London.

As for the laity, in general they are advised only to practise daily meditation, always at the same time and in the same place.

A Buddhist monk of Scottish origin justified this advice as follows:

'We know how quickly the habit of doing the same thing at the same time is acquired. He who is accustomed to walk or to eat at a fixed time feels, automatically, the desire to go out, or the need to eat, precisely at this time. This tendency, which is very strong, can help us in the practice of meditation. When we have devoted, regularly, a certain time to meditation, at a fixed hour of the day, the habit is established, and concentration becomes easier.

'A similar effect is obtained by meditating in a special place, and always the same place.

'A merchant may have his mind full of worries, but when he re-enters his shop or his office the thoughts connected with his business easily take the upper hand. It is the same with a doctor, who, suddenly awakened from sleep, is in full possession of his professional perspicuity the moment he is at the patient's bedside. It is the same with the captain of a ship on his bridge, with the chemist in his laboratory, etc.; the habit of a special mental attitude in a certain place acts mechanically on them. Even apart from any professional routine, our attitude, and the course of our ideas, are modified according to the place wherein we find ourselves. This modification is due not only to the impression made

upon us by the external appearance of this place, but
also to the ideas which we are accustomed to attach to
it, to the general idea which those about us have of it,
to the feelings which we ourselves and others have
experienced in this place. A temple, a monastery, a
theatre, a tea-room, the deck of a passenger steamer,
excite in us different tendencies, and inspire the manifestation of different aspects of our personality. A special
place to which one resorts only in order to devote oneself
to meditation will more readily incline the mind to
recollection, through the effect of acquired habit, and
the order of thoughts which the sight of it, and its own
peculiar atmosphere, will awaken in us.'[1]

Here again the puritans of Buddhism raise objections.
The observations of this author are perfectly correct,
but are not the influences on which he relies in order
to produce a certain state of mind a kind of suggestion,
and consequently, are not the sentiments which they evoke
artificial? That a man entering into his place of meditation and seating himself in his accustomed chair feels
suddenly invested with calm and serenity, does not mean
that if on leaving his place of meditation he should meet
persons who are occupied in doing him injury he will
preserve this same calm, this same serenity. Yet this is
the only thing that matters.

All Buddhists who habitually practise meditation
know the sensation of peace, of delicious detachment,
experienced when one is preparing to meditate. The

[1] *On the Culture of Mind,* by Ananda Maitriya (Allan Bennett).

Tibetans give it an expressive name, *niamparjagpa*;[1] that is, 'allowing to equal' or 'making equal', and this is explained by the simile of the sea of which all the waves are flattened out, and which becomes smooth as a mirror.

Although the sentiments which may arise in such a state of mind, if this is artificially produced, may themselves be artificial, yet very many Buddhists consider that this calm, this temporary detachment, is not without its results. One of these results is to produce a salutary relaxation, not only of the mind, but of the whole organism. After these periods of rest the disciple finds himself more alert and more spiritually energetic.

It should be noted that the *Jhânas*, like all meditations tending to produce certain sentiments in the mind of the disciple, are considered to be of far less value than the practice of *Attention*. This latter alone is believed to lead to Nirvâna. The meditations, at best, only serve to purify the mind, and to create favourable conditions for the practice of *Right Attention*.

Besides the *Jhânas* which have been described above, Buddhists mention four others, of a higher kind, which they call *arûpa jhânas*—'contemplations without form'— so as to distinguish them from the others, which are *rûpa jhânas*—that is to say, meditations related to the world of 'form'.

When the disciple has attained to perfect serenity, when he has put an end to the sensations of pleasure

[1] Written *mnam par bshag pa*.

and of pain, and has rejected the joy and the suffering which he has felt in the past (which is effected by completely detaching his mind from the sentiments provoked by the memories which they have left with him), he is qualified to advance beyond the world of phenomena (the world of form).

'He has suppressed the ideas which relate to form. He has suppressed the perception of the objects of sense, such as forms, sounds, odours, taste, and touch by contact with the body; in this way he has suppressed the ideas relating to all kinds of contacts. He has suppressed the ideas of classification, of distinction and multiplicity. He thinks: "Space is infinite". Thinking thus, the disciple attains the region of infinite space and remains there. This is the *first of the contemplations without form.*

'After suppressing the region of infinite space, the disciple thinks: "Consciousness is infinite." Thinking thus, he attains the region of infinite consciousness and remains there. This is the *second of the contemplations without form.*

'After suppressing the region of infinite consciousness, the disciple thinks: "There is nothing there." Thinking thus, he attains the region of the void (the region where nothing exists), and remains there. This is the *third of the contemplations without form.*

'After suppressing the region of the void, the disciple attains the region where there are neither ideas nor the absence of ideas. This is the *fourth of the contemplations without form.*'

This description, which is somewhat obscure for us, is much more intelligible to Orientals, who read it in the Sanskrit, Pali, or Tibetan texts, and who are familiar with terms for which we possess no exact equivalent. 'Region' is an indifferent approximation for *ayatana*, which means 'dwelling', 'inner seat', translated by Professor Stcherbatsky as 'entry'; all these are expressions needing elucidation. In fact, the *ârupa jhânas* correspond to a succession of states of mind, to a progression of thought beyond the world of form and phenomena.

The *infinity of space* is perceived when one has ceased to subdivide it by distinguishing separate things in it, when one has banished from one's mind the idea of multiplicity.

The *infinity of consciousness* is perceived when one ceases to imprison the consciousness within the limits of the sensations and perceptions which are communicated to it by the senses as they make contact with exterior objects. According to the Dzogstchenpas (a Tibetan sect) the idea of the infinity of consciousness follows after that of the infinity of space because this latter is recognized as existing *in* the consciousness and not outside it.

The *void, non-existence*, are perceived when, after having minutely examined and analysed all the *dharmas* (elements of existence, phenomena), one has recognized them as impermanent and as having no 'self'. Non-existence is also the absence of all that makes up the world as it appears to those whose perceptions is obscured by the fetters[1] and by the obstacles.[2]

That which follows the suppression of all ideas begotten by the contact of the senses with the objects which make up the world of form (these objects having been expelled from the field of consciousness) can be defined only as a 'region' in which there are no ideas. But from the fact that this *kind* of ideas is suppressed, ought one to conclude that there is a total absence of ideas of *another kind*? Evidently those who defined the *arupa jhâna* did not so intend, for they declared that in this fourth contemplation there were *neither ideas nor absence of ideas*. We may understand this as describing a transcendent state which corresponds to nothing that can be expressed in words.

It is said that the disciple passes gradually from one to another of these contemplations, but progress may be slow. It is not in the space of an hour or of a day that one can travel from the 'region of infinite space' to that in which 'one ceases to have ideas, and where, none the less, one is not without them'. This may happen to highly trained individuals, but beginners sometimes require years to accomplish this philosophical pilgrimage. Those who boast of doing it quickly are deceiving themselves and have understood nothing of the nature of the

[1] The Fetters are: Self-illusion (belief in the permanent *ego*), Doubt, Belief in the efficacy of religious rites, Desire for a future life, whether in our world (the world of sensuality) or in the world of pure form, or in the formless world, Pride, Ignorance.

[2] The obstacles are: Presumption, Lust, Anger, Indifference, Mental Agitation, Doubt.

*jhânas.* Such, at least, is the opinion of Buddhists who practise these contemplations seriously.

Not all Buddhists regard the *arupa jhânas* as four successive stages. There are some who consider that one may attain directly to any one of them, and that it is possible to reach the state of mind represented by one or other of the *jhânas* without being capable of attaining another.

It goes without saying that these contemplations have been the subject of numerous commentaries. There is nothing specifically Buddhistic about them, and they have been partially borrowed from the School of Yoga. It should be noted that in Buddhism they are regarded as accessories, practices which may be useful but which are in no way indispensable for salvation, which is of the intellectual order, and depends on the acquisition of knowledge. Here I must repeat what I have said regarding the lower jhânas: They cannot, in any case, replace the practice of *Attention*.

The kind of meditation which follows, and which is practised in Tibet, is derived from a conception which is shared by the adepts of the sect which is described, *par excellence*, as the 'sect of meditation', known as Ts'an in China, and Zen in Japan; the most singular, and in many ways the most remarkable, of the Buddhist sects. According to this conception, the mind 'in its natural state' perceives Reality. What prevents it from perceiving Reality is the continual outflow of ideas which disturb it, making it like water ruffled by the wind, in which objects are not clearly reflected, and all images are distorted. This illustration is classic:

'When one meditates,' we are told, 'one perceives that ideas arise one from the other, in great numbers, and with extreme rapidity. It is necessary then, as soon as a thought begins to form, to cut it off at the root and to continue one's meditation.

'Continuing the meditation, and gradually prolonging the length of the periods during which the formation of ideas is inhibited, one ends by realizing that, by the very fact of this involuntary formation of ideas, the latter succeed one another, tread on one another's heels, and form an interminable procession.

'This discovery of the *involuntary* formation of ideas is equivalent to the discovery of enemies.

'The condition which one has then attained resembles that of a man who, from the river bank, watches the water flow past. Even so the mind, observant and calm, watches the passing of the uninterrupted flux of ideas which hurry after one another.

'If the mind attains to this state, even if only for a moment, it understands the birth and the creation of mental formations.

'That which is outside the birth of mental formations (samskâras), and which instantly puts an end to the latter, is Reality.'[1]

This last statement is akin to another which we find

---

[1] From the *Chag Chen gyi zindi*, written: *phyag chen gyi zin bris*, a Tibetan treatise.

in the Dhammapada: 'When thou hast understood the dissolution of all formations (samskâra) thou shalt understand *that* which is unformed.'

Does all this mean that the disciple will become omniscient, that he will discover the secret of eternity and of the infinite? We must not think this. It is rather a question of realizing the unreality of the imaginary world which is created around us by the ideas which we entertain, or which arise spontaneously in us without the cooperation of our will, or even against it.

### EFFORT AND WILL

The Buddhist Scriptures mention four sorts of effort:

(1) *Effort to avoid*—To endeavour to prevent harmful or false ideas which one has never entertained from entering the mind. To endeavour not to commit harmful actions which one has never yet committed.

(2) *Effort to dominate.*—To endeavour to reject, to annihilate, the evil tendencies which one feels in oneself. Not to let them take root. To combat covetousness, anger, illusion; to conquer and reject them.

There are five methods of getting rid of harmful thoughts: (*a*) Oppose a salutary idea to the harmful one; (*b*) Consider the pernicious effects of the harmful idea; (*c*) Pay no attention to it; (*d*) Analyse it, discover the elements which constitute it, and the causes which beget it; (*e*) Arm oneself with a strong will, and do violence to oneself.

(3) *Effort to acquire.*—To endeavour to cultivate in

oneself all the salutary tendencies which one does not yet possess. To acquire the qualities requisite to attain to Wisdom; that is to say: attention, penetration, energy, interest, tranquillity, concentration of mind, and equanimity.

(4) *Effort to maintain.*—To endeavour to preserve the salutary tendencies and ideas which one possesses; not to let them grow weaker or disappear; to work at their development and to bring them to perfection.

Effort, in short, however it may be directed, aims at preparing the field so that Wisdom may be implanted there. According to the Buddhist Scriptures, it seems that indolence is the most serious enemy of wisdom and of knowledge, and the disciple is specially urged to fight against it.

'Wisdom is acquired by means of effort; it is lost by indifference. Attentively consider the twofold path of growth and of loss, and choose the path on which wisdom grows and increases.' (Dhammapada.)

'The true disciple has rejected apathy and idleness; he is delivered from them. Loving the light, intelligent, clear-minded, he purges himself of all apathy, all idleness.' (Majjahima Sutta.)

'We fight, and that is why we call ourselves warriors. We fight for the highest virtue, for an exalted aim, for sublime wisdom.' (Anguttara Nikâya.)

'The wise man should not halt after a first step; he should march forward ceaselessly toward a more complete knowledge.' (Fo-sho-king-tsang-king.)

The effort which we have just been considering presupposed the previous existence of the will. This, however, is presented as a special 'branch' of the *Path*, because it includes not only the perfection of the will, which becomes inflexible and persevering, but also the perfection of the goal at which this will is aiming.

Right resolve (or perfect will) must be liberated from three categories of thoughts: those of ill will, those of cruelty, and those directed towards sensuality.

Right resolve is directed toward a twofold aim, the personal and the altruistic.

*The personal aim*: to acquire Knowledge.

'Vigorous and alert, such is the disciple; his powers are well-balanced, he is neither immoderately ardent, nor given over to ease. And he is filled with this thought: "May my skin, my muscles, my nerves, my bones, and my blood dry up rather than that I should renounce my efforts before having attained all that which can be attained by human power and perseverance." (Majjhima Nikâya.) The Buddha, according to tradition, pronounced these words before seating himself under the Bo-tree, at the foot of which he attained spiritual illumination.

'Turn not aside from that which you have decided. When you have attained your goal, attach yourselves firmly to it.' (Dhammapada.)

And the goal of the Buddhist is deliverance from error, from ignorance, the cause of covetousness and anger; it is the unshakable deliverance of the mind which has attained to peace by Knowledge.

### THE ALTRUISTIC AIM

In the mind of the disciple an immense compassion is born. He has seen and understood the lamentable fate of the beings dragged from all eternity, by the round of rebirths, from suffering to suffering, and the resolve to lighten their sufferings and to liberate them from them forces itself upon him.

Can we be certain, we may ask, that the connection between the knowledge of the fact of another's suffering and the desire to deliver him from it is rigorously logical and inevitable? Assuredly, nothing is less certain if we reason on the basis of our egoistical conception of the personality, understood as a unity entirely distinct and separated from other personalities. But from the different standpoint to which the disciple is translated by his comprehension of the universal impermanence, and the non-existence of the 'ego', Buddhists declare that the connection is normal.

Without discussing the reasonableness of such a statement, we may doubtless hold that this intellectual compassion, which is peculiar to Buddhism, is the sign denoting those who are fit to become the disciples of the Buddha. One day the lamentable distress of all that lives has appeared to them. Without being dominated by unreasonable emotion, which Buddhism proscribes, but maintaining their composure, they have seen clearly the confusion of the crowds that run after pleasure, stretching forth their hands toward the mocking mirage of a happiness which always flees toward the distant future, from which nothing can come save the hideous spectre of death. They have contemplated the effect of the stupidity and the passions which set men against one another, like imprisoned wild beasts which kill one another through the bars of their cage. Before this misery, this suffering, which, under the indifferent sky, has repeated itself since the beginning of time, they are seized with an immense pity.

Thus a reasoned war against all forms of suffering, and for the welfare of all beings, is the second aspect of Right Resolve applied to the proper aim.

'All beings seek for happiness; so let your compassion extend itself to all.' (Mahâvamsa.)

On a pillar which the Emperor Asoka set up for the edification of his subjects, one read: 'I consider the welfare of beings as an aim for which I must strive.'

The Mahâyânists have insisted strongly on the precept of charity and of love for living creatures; they have made it the basis of their popular teaching, sometimes falling, unfortunately, into absurd exaggerations. It would, however, be unjust to reserve all our strictures for the Mahâyânists alone, for the Hinayânists also do not fail to admire the extravagant and ridiculous deeds of imaginary heroes borrowed from the Hindu tales.

Such a hero is Vessantara, a young prince who made a vow to practise perfect charity by giving anything for which he was asked. Being regent of his father's kingdom in the absence of the latter, not only did he empty the treasury by his continual gifts, but he gave to an enemy prince the war-elephants and the magic jewel which assured its possessor of victory. Having carried off this marvellous talisman, the enemy prince attacked the country of the over-charitable hero, pillaged it, put it to the sword, and massacred the inhabitants.

When we learn that the unhappy saint was banished in punishment for his acts, we applaud this just judgement. Not so the Asiatics who hear this story, to whom he appears as an infinitely touching and admirable victim.

Now Prince Vessantara was exiled, and lived in the forest with his wife and their two children.[1] One day when he was alone with the children, their mother having gone to search for wild fruit, an old Brahmin arrived unexpectedly. He explained to the exile that since age had robbed him of his strength he needed servants to take care of him. These servants might be the son and daughter[2] of Vessantara; let the prince give them to him as slaves. The charitable prince did not hesitate for a moment; delighted that he was able to accomplish so meritorious a sacrifice, he gave his children to the old man.

The children, however, having managed to escape, returned to their parents. This time their mother was present; but deaf to her prayers, Vessantara did not hesitate to restore his son and daughter to the old Brahmin, who, coming to reclaim them, bound them

[1] This is a favourite theme of Hindu stories. Râma lived in the forest with his wife Sîta; Kunala, with his wife, wandered as a beggar.

[2] In the Tibetan version of this tale the children are three, two boys and a girl.

and beat them before the eyes of their father, who was absorbed in his dream of perfect charity.

Later, in the same way, he gave his wife. Then, to crown all, he tore out his own eyes to give them to a blind man, who from that moment could see.

On several occasions I have vainly tried to explain the immoral character of this story to Orientals who nourished their strange piety upon it. How could charity go hand in hand with sufferings inflicted on those whom the most sacred obligations command us to protect? This seems incomprehensible to us, but the point of view of the authors of these tales is the very antipodes of ours. For them, wife and children are the property of the head of the family, on the same footing as his dog or his jewels. 'To give the most precious thing one has,' so I have been answered, 'is an act of the greatest charity.' To this we agree, but the donor should give only what belongs to him, and long ago we outgrew the barbarous conceptions that regard wife and children as the property of the husband. However, since more humane ideas have made their way into the countries where such fables are current, there are many who see the shocking side of them, and appease their instinctive feelings of disapproval by saying that the victims, wife and children, consented to sacrifice themselves. But there still remains the fact that the prince had treacherously stolen the talisman on which depended the prosperity and the safety of his countrymen, and had delivered it into the hands of their enemy.

Dragged down to this level by the ignorant and super-stitious masses who embraced it centuries ago, and who continue today to confess it without ever having under-stood its teaching, Buddhism has assumed an unexpected form. This exuberance of charitable sentiment readily becomes egoism. If Vessantara and those like him practise giving without regard for the sufferings which they cause, it is in the hope that this discipline, continued through many successive lives, will lead them to become a Buddha, capable of showing to living beings the Way that leads to the deliverance from suffering. A strange idea, to begin by causing suffering in order to attain such a goal.

But, as I have said, the Orientals regard these tales from another point of view than ours; moreover, it would be easy for them to find in the West the counterpart of these irrational phantasies.

We must also note that the good sense and feeling for justice of the good people among whom these tales are held in honour have led them to make certain improve-ments. The wicked old Brahmin is held to be a disguised god, who wished to test the firmness of Vessantara's resolve. At the end of the tale his children, his wife, and even his eyes are restored to him. He is recalled to his country. Moreover, the enemy prince restores the magic jewel and rebuilds the towns which he had destroyed, and the two countries become allies. The same treatment has been applied to other stories of this kind.

A much pleasanter story concerning charity is that of the hare.

It is the day of full moon (a Buddhist festival, like a monthly Sunday) and the wise hare thinks: Today it is fitting to practise charity, but if someone comes to me, what can I give him? I have neither beans nor rice nor butter; I eat nothing but grass; one cannot give grass. But I know what I will do, I will give myself in charity.

It happened, as is usual in these fables, that a god wished to test the wise hare. He came to him in the form of a Brahmin. When the hare saw him he cried joyously: 'Thou dost well, O Brahmin, to come to ask me for food. I will give thee such a gift as has never yet been given. Thou leadest a pure life and thou wouldst not do harm to a living being. But collect wood and light a great fire; I will roast myself so that thou canst eat.'

'It is well,' replied the Brahmin, 'so be it.' With joy he collected wood and heaped it up in a pile in the middle of which he placed some burning embers. Soon a great fire was blazing, and the Brahmin seated himself by it. Then the wise hare, with one bound, leapt into the middle of the flames. Hair and hide, flesh and nerves, bones and heart, he had given his whole body.'[1]

Besides the incredible stories designed to exalt immoderate charity, there are some of great dramatic

[1] But according to another version: 'The flames were cool to the saintly hare, the fire did not even touch one hair of its body. The Brahmin-god placed it on fresh grass, and to perpetuate the memory of the charitable hare he squeezed a mountain, and using its juice as paint, he painted the figure of a hare on the moon.'

beauty. Here, in my opinion, is the most striking of
them.

A young prince (said to be the historical Buddha in
one of his previous existences) is travelling through a
forest. An abnormal drought has dried up the springs;
the river-beds are nothing but sand and stones; the leaves,
calcined by a blazing sun, fall into dust, and the animals
have fled elsewhere. There, in the midst of this desolation,
the prince sees, close to him, in a thicket, a famished and
dying tigress surrounded by her young. The beast sees
him too, and her eyes blaze with her ardent longing to
hurl herself upon this prey, so close to her, and to feed
her young with it, her young that she can no longer
suckle, and who like her will die of starvation. But she
lacks the strength to rise and leap at him . . . she remains
outstretched, pitiable in her maternal distress and her
longing for life.

Then the young prince, with perfect composure and
calm compassion, turns aside from his path, and approach-
ing the tigress, who could not reach him, he gives himself
to her as food.

The beauty of this story is that it disdains the usual
final miracle. No god intervenes; the prince is devoured,
and the curtain falls on the mystery of what may
follow.

This is probably a mere legend, with no historical
foundation; yet I believe—not entirely without reason—
that an action of this kind might really have been accomplished. It is difficult to plumb the depths of charity and

detachment to which certain Buddhist mystics have attained.

Apart from such tales as this last, which reflect quite exceptional feelings, one sees in the examples illustrating the popular teaching, whether Hinâyânist or Mahâyânist, a strange forgetfulness of the fundamental principles of Buddhism. According to these latter, Right Views are an indispensable guide to whomsoever wishes to labour efficaciously for the well-being, either spiritual or material, of his neighbour.

A Hindu saying tells us that 'in order to draw a man out of a quicksand in which he is embedded, one must have one's feet on solid ground'. How can a blind man who does not see the precipice toward which a traveller is walking warn him in time to prevent his fall?

Thus the Right Resolve is, always, above all, to acquire Right Views, which is the aim toward which the whole Buddhist programme of moral training tends.


RIGHT VIEWS

According to a tradition which is accepted by all Buddhist sects, Siddharta Gautama, after attaining spiritual illumination, went to Benares. He knew that at a short distance from the town, in a park known as the 'Park of the Gazelles' (Mrigadava), dwelt five ascetics, formerly fellow-disciples of his, who had followed the same philosophic quest as himself, a quest whose goal he believed he had now attained. No one, he thought, would be better able than these men to understand what he had discovered: the 'Middle Way' which leads to freedom from suffering.

The sermon which he preached to them is included in the oldest Buddhist texts, and we have every reason to believe that it was actually spoken by the Buddha if not word for word, as we have it, at least with the same significance. Here is a summary of his sermon:

'Hear!' said the Buddha. 'The Eternal is found (eternal, as opposed to impermanence; more literally, death-less).[1] I will teach you the Doctrine. If you follow the way which I show you, in a little while you will attain that high goal for the sake of which youths of noble families abandon their homes and lead the life of wandering ascetics. In this very life you will possess the Truth, knowing it and seeing it face to face.

'There are two extremes which he who would lead a spiritual life should avoid. One is a life given up to sensuality, to enjoyment; this is degrading, vulgar, contrary to the spirit, and profitless. The other is a life of mortification; this is painful, unworthy and profitless. The Tathâgata (the Buddha) has kept aloof from these two extremes; he has found the middle path which unseals the eyes and the mind, which leads to wisdom, to tranquillity, to enlightenment, to Nirvâna.

'It is the Noble Eightfold Path, the Path with eight branches, which are: Right Views, Right Resolve, Right Speech, Right Conduct, Right Livelihood, Right Effort, Right Attention, Right Meditation.'

[1] *Amrita.*

Then the Buddha expounded to the five ascetics the Twelve Interpedendent Origins (Pratîtyasamûtpâda) which were the subject of the preceding chapter.

Thus, in his first sermon the Buddha offered his hearers a method of mental training, assuring them that its practise would enable them to *see* the truth, and thus to possess right views.

Did the Buddha point out to his disciples what constituted 'Right Views'? To do so might seem to be superfluous, since the Master had stated to them that if they followed the way which he showed them (the Eightfold Path) they would themselves see the truth face to face. In any case, it is certain that in the course of his fifty years of teaching the Buddha did not fail to expound those 'views' which he held to be correct. The echo of declarations of this kind comes to us in the oldest *sûtras*, but the impression which they leave on us is that the Buddha bade his disciples endeavour to acquire Right Views, and that except for a few essential points he abstained from any precise statement of the 'views' which he himself considered 'right'.

Perhaps he feared that overmuch insistence on his own beliefs might lead some of his disciples to *believe* that which he believed, out of respect for his words, instead of *seeing* because 'the dust which covered their spiritual eye' (Mahâvagga) had been removed. Yet another reason might incline Gautama to refrain from confiding to his disciples all that he personally believed. He judged, no doubt, that many of his beliefs, based on his own perceptions, could have neither value nor real utility for those who lacked the same reason to believe. A passage of the *Samyutta-Nikâya* confirms this opinion. Here is what it says:

'One day Bhavagad (the Venerable—a title of respect) was dwelling at Kausambi in the forest of sinsapa-trees. And the Venerable One took a few sinsapa-leaves in his hand, and said to the disciples: Which, think you, are the most numerous, these few sinsapa-leaves which I hold in my hand, or the other leaves which are overhead in the forest of sinsapa-trees?

'—These leaves which the Venerable One holds in his hand are few in number, far greater in number are those which are above us in the wood.

'—Even so, O disciples, the things which I have discovered and have not told you are more numerous than those which I have told you. And why have I not told them to you?—Because these things would not bring you any profit. They would not lead you to detachment from earthly things, to the extinction of desire, to peace, to knowledge, to Nirvâna.'

Thus, what the Buddha kept to himself was not knowledge superior to that which he publicly expounded, but details of the nature of commentaries on 'Right Views', or, perhaps, incommunicable perceptions which others could not utilize. The idea of an esoteric doctrine, reserved for an élite, is completely unknown to primitive Buddhism. It is impossible to insist too strongly on this point, for in the West many erroneous views have been propagated in this connection.

The esotericism which one finds in certain branches of the Mahâyâna is due to the incorporation in them of Tantric doctrines. But it should be understood that this esotericism is concerned with the teaching of particular methods, relating to physiology, psychology, and magic, and not in any way with transcendent truths. An esoteric doctrine would be in opposition to the declaration already quoted: 'If you follow the way which I show you, in this very life you will perceive the truth, knowing it and seeing it face to face.' So soon as there exists a means of *knowing* and *seeing* for oneself, secrecy is futile and the initiator superfluous.

We have seen what is, for the Buddhist, the first Right View. It is that which arouses the belief in the beneficent effects of the discipline of the Path, and leads to its practice, at least, as an experiment. After this the nature of the Right Views differs according to the intellectual capacity of the traveller on the Path. It should be noted that Right Views are by no means dogmas, and that at the beginning of the Buddhist's spiritual training to 'see right' is not necessarily to comprehend Absolute Truth (which is, for that matter, always incomprehensible). In this case to 'see right' is to govern oneself reasonably, to seek, by study, attention, and assiduous investigation, the conquest of Knowledge.

Buddhists conceive Right Views, and the whole of the Path based upon them, as existing on two different planes:

the plane which 'belongs to the world' (lokya) and the plane which is 'beyond the world' (lokuttara). We may regard the first of these as a path for the use of disciples of ordinary virtue and intelligence, who are simply aiming at happy rebirths, either on this earth or in the various paradises. The second is the Way on which travel those disciples who are endowed with highly developed intellectual faculties, whose will to attain enlightenment is firm and unflinching. Actually, only these latter ought to be regarded as being truly Buddhists. Symbolically they are said to have 'entered the stream, because just as the water of a river never runs backwards toward its source, but flows steadily and inevitably toward the ocean, so, more or less rapidly, but with certainty, these disciples will attain to Enlightenment.'

He enters the stream who is delivered from: (1) the delusion which leads to the belief in the existence in us of a permanent and non-compounded 'ego'; (2) doubts concerning the Causes of Suffering and the Way which leads to its destruction; (3) faith in the efficacy of religious rites.

But it must be clearly understood that this triple deliverance is the fruit of the investigations and reflections of the disciple himself; an acceptance 'on faith' would be worthless.

A number of passages in the Buddhist Scriptures attribute to the Buddha declarations enjoining his disciples to base their beliefs on personal research and examination, and to accept the theories which he put before them only after they had recognized for themselves that these theories corresponded with the facts.

'One day the Buddha, passing through the country of the princes of Kalama, was interrogated by them: "Lord", they said to him, "the Brahmins and the leaders of sects come among us, and each of them solemnly affirms that only that which he teaches is true, and that all else is naught but error. It follows, Lord, that doubt has arisen among us, and that we no longer know what doctrine to accept." '

The Buddha replied: 'It is in the nature of things that doubt should arise.'

And he counselled them to believe nothing which was merely based on the statements of others.

'Do not put faith in traditions, even though they have been accepted for long generations and in many countries. Do not believe a thing because many repeat it. Do not accept a thing on the authority of one or another of the Sages of old, nor on the ground that a statement is found in the books. Never believe anything because probability is in its favour. Do not believe in that which you have yourselves imagined, thinking that a god has inspired it. Believe nothing merely on the authority of your teachers or of the priests. After examination, believe that which you have tested for yourselves and found reasonable, which is in conformity with your well-being and that of others.' (Kâlâma Sutta.)

Elsewhere, after having discoursed with his disciples on the Law of Causality, the Buddha concluded:

'. . . If, now, you understand thus and see thus, will you say: "We venerate the Master, and out of respect for him, we speak thus?"—"Lord, we will not do so."—"That which you say, O disciples, is it not only that which you have yourselves seen, yourselves recognized yourselves understood?"—"It is so, O Lord." ' (Majjhima Nikâya.)

In our inquiry we may, as did the Buddha, address ourselves to various masters, listen to their teachings, and study different doctrines. It is good to do so; certain Mahâyânists, long after the time of the Buddha, said that it was even indispensable; but, in the long run, the light which is really capable of illuminating our path must come from ourselves.

'Shine for thyself, as thine own light.' (Dhammapada.)

'Be your own torch. Be your own refuge. Confide in no refuge outside yourselves. Hold fast to the truth, that it may be your torch. Hold fast to the truth, that it may be your refuge. Seek safety in none but yourselves. . . . Those, O Ananda, who from today or after my death shall be their own torch and their own refuge, who, holding fast to the truth, value it for their torch and their refuge—these will be the first among my disciples; they will attain the supreme end.'

According to the *Mahâparinibbâna Sutta*, these words were among the exhortations which the Buddha addressed to his disciples during the last days of his life.

The canonical writings often show us the Buddha as an enemy of metaphysical theories. Man's researches, he

hinks, should be carried out within the limits attainable
by his perceptions; to wish to go beyond this solid
ground is to fall into disastrous errors. At the best, it is to
waste time which could have been employed in acquiring
knowledge of service in fighting and destroying suffering.

'O disciple, do not entertain thoughts of this kind:
The world is eternal. The world is not eternal. The world
is limited. The world is infinite. Whether the world is
eternal or not, whether it is limited or infinite, what is
certain is that birth, old age, death, and suffering exist.'
Samyutta Nikâya and Majjhima Nikâya.)

Useless, also, are all discussions concerning existence
and non-existence.

'The world is accustomed to postulate a duality:
existence and non-existence. But he who perceives, in
truth and in wisdom, how things arise and cease in the
world, for such a one there is neither existence nor non-
existence.' (Samyutta Nikâya.)

The Buddhist Scriptures of the Theravadins show the
Buddha as a master who bases his doctrine solely on
facts whose reality is clear to him. He says of himself
that he is exempt from all theories. If anyone asks of one
of his disciples: 'Does the Master Gautama hold such and
such an opinion?' the reply should be: 'The Master is
exempt from all theories. . . . He has won complete
deliverance by rejecting all opinions and all hypo-
theses. . . .' (Majjhima Nikâya.)

The Buddha was careful, for that matter, to deny that
his teaching had the character of a revelation. He was

merely a man who could see farther than others, and could show these others what he had seen, so that they, in their turn, could see it. The existence of a Buddha is in no way indispensable; it cannot alter facts.

'Whether Buddhas appear in the world or whether they do not appear, the fact remains that all things are impermanent, are subject to suffering, and that none of them (no phenomenon) constitutes an "ego."' (Anguttara Nikâya.)

With this last statement we reach the fundamental doctrine of Buddhism.

'All aggregations are impermanent.

'All aggregations are suffering.

'All the constitutive elements of existence are devoid of "ego."'

Such is the *credo* of Buddhism, and the adepts of all its sects, whether Hinayânist or Mahâyânist, adhere unanimously to these three affirmations. Let us remember, however, that this *credo* is not put forward as an *article of faith* but as a subject to be *examined* by Buddhists. These latter having been warned against the danger of giving themselves up to their own imagination in attacking problems whose solution is beyond the power of their means of perception, the field of research which is suggested to them consists in their own person and in the phenomena which arise around them.

How do Buddhists regard the person?—They see it as composed of five parts which they call *skandhas*: material

form (the body), sensations, perceptions, mental formations (ideas, volitions, etc.) and consciousness.

'In the absolute sense, there is no individual, no person;
what exists is merely these perpetually changing combinations of physical conditions, sensations, perceptions,
volitions, and phases of consciousness. Just as that which
we indicate by the name of "chariot" has no existence
apart from axle, wheels, shafts, body, and so forth; or
as the word "house" is merely a convenient designation
for stone, wood, lime, iron, and so on, assembled after
a certain fashion so as to enclose a portion of space, and
there is no separate house-entity in existence; in exactly
the same way that which we call a being, or an individual,
or a person, or describe as "I", is nothing but a changing
combination of physical and psychical phenomena, and
has no real existence in itself.

'Individual, person, man, "I", are merely terms useful to
employ in current speech, to which, however, nothing in
reality corresponds. For none of the physical and mental
phenomena which make up a being constitute an absolute
-entity, and apart from these phenomena there is no I-
entity who is the master, the possessor of these phenomena.

'Hence, when in the Buddhist texts, as is frequently
the case, mention is made of a person, or even of the
rebirth of a person, this is simply a manner of expressing
oneself more easily. The absolute truth, however, is this
—that the so-called *being* is merely a perpetually changing
process of the five Aggregates of Existence.'[1]

[1] Nyanatiloka: *The Word of the Buddha.*

Each of the five parts which constitute the person is itself compounded. The physical form draws its substance from the elements denominated, in the Buddhist treatises, the solid, the fluid, heat, and the moving, and symbolized as earth, water, fire, and wind. They are also regarded as the four elemental forces: inertia, cohesion, radiation, and vibration.

Expressing themselves in a more familiar manner, contemporary Buddhists say: the body is formed from a first supply of matter furnished by the parents; then, when the child is born, he adds to his physical form by assimilating the food which he eats. And so, continually, while life lasts, the existence of the body depends on nourishment. This body, then, has no real, personal existence; it is nothing but a product of the transformation of the aliments.

Nor can the 'I' be located in one or other of the four elements of the 'person' which form his mental part: sensations—perceptions—mental formations—consciousness; none of those exists by itself. Sensations and perceptions depend on the senses and on their respective objects. The ideas, the volitions, all the operations of the mind, depend on the perceptions, on the sensations, which furnish it with the materials that nourish its activity. Consciousness[1] depends on causes; of what would one be conscious if sensations, perceptions, and ideas were lacking?—And just as the body is nothing but substance

---

[1] The term 'consciousness' is always understood by the Buddhists as 'the fact of being conscious' of something.

borrowed from without, and has no existence of its own, apart from the first supply of matter furnished by the parents and the foodstuffs which have preserved and increased its flesh, its blood, its bones, etc., so also the mental part of the individual is constituted from supplies from without which reach it by means of the five senses and the mind, which is regarded as a sixth sense whose object is ideas. Thus one seeks in vain in the physical or mental part of the individual for an element which is not dependent on something else, which exists by itself, independent and self-produced, unconnected with anything else, as a veritable 'I' should be.

Is it possible to imagine a 'person' who had neither physical form, nor sensations, nor perceptions, nor ideas, nor states of consciousness? Where would be the 'person' apart from all these? When the faithful of different religions speak of a soul, this latter is represented as being formed of all that constitutes the mental part of the man, i.e. sensations, perceptions, ideas, states of consciousness. And all these elements of a 'person' spring from causes, derive their existence from outside elements, are nothing but the momentary form of a combination of causes and elements, and therefore, are not an 'I', and the 'person', immaterial as well as the material, constituted by the assemblage of these elements, cannot, in any way, be regarded as an 'I'.

'In the absolute sense (paramartha-vasena) there exist only innumerable processes, an infinity of waves in the sea, always in movement, of forms, sensations, perceptions, tendencies, and states of consciousness; none of these perpetually changing phenomena constitutes a permanent entity which can be called "I" or a "*me*", and there exists no *ego*-entity outside of them.'[1]

After having heard what a very orthodox Theravadin has to say, let us now listen to a Mahâyânist lama.

The following parable will give some idea of the way in which the Tibetan masters express themselves when their lessons are put in a simple form. It is required to describe what is a 'person', in the physical and the mental sense. But according to the Tibetans there is no distinct line of demarcation between the physical and the mental. All physical phenomena relating to the 'person' have, among the causes which produce them, causes of a mental kind, and all mental phenomena have, among the causes to which they are due, some causes of a physical kind.

Here is the parable:

A 'person' resembles an assembly composed of a number of members. In this assembly discussion never ceases. Now and again one of the members rises, makes a speech, and suggests an action; his colleagues approve, and it is decided that what he has proposed shall be executed. Or now several members of the assembly rise at the same time and propose different things, and each of them, for private reasons, supports his own proposal. It may happen that these differences of opinion, and the passion which each of the orators brings into the debate,

[1] Nyanatiloka: *The Word of the Buddha.*

will provoke a quarrel, even a violent quarrel, in the assembly. Fellow-members may even come to blows.

It also happens that some members of the assembly leave it of their own accord; others are gradually pushed out, and others again are expelled by force, by their colleagues. All this time newcomers introduce themselves into the assembly, either by gently sidling in or by forcing the doors.

Again, one notes that certain members of the assembly are slowly perishing; their voices become feeble, and finally they are no longer heard. Others, on the contrary, who were weak and timid, become stronger and bolder; they become violent, shouting their proposals; they terrify their colleagues, and dominate them, and end by making themselves dictators.

The members of this assembly are the physical and mental elements which constitute the 'person'; they are our instincts, our tendencies, our ideas, our beliefs, our desires, etc. Through the causes which engendered it, each of them is the descendant and heir of many lines of causes, of many series of phenomena, going far back into the past, and whose traces are lost in the shadowy depths of eternity.

It is thus that the psychologists of Tibet explain the contradictory tendencies of which we are conscious, and also our gradual or sudden changes of opinion and of conduct. Both one and the other depend on the temporary composition of the assembly which is the

'person', the 'I', and on the character of the members
who are for the time being in the majority, and elect its
president.

Is there, among Buddhists, the same unanimity concerning the nature of the world as is manifested in respect
of the nature of the person ?—It is impossible to reply in
the affirmative, and, in spite of all appearances, it would
be unwise to reply with a categorical negative. Oriental
thinkers are desperately subtle. We run a serious risk of
misunderstanding their thought if we have only books
for guides. It is often useful to supplement the study of
the Buddhist canonical texts by the commentaries
furnished by educated, living Buddhists, who, by a long
intellectual heredity, and also, no doubt, by certain
dispositions peculiar to the Asiatics, are more capable
than ourselves of understanding the exact sense of statements whose terms have no equivalent in our languages,
and do not correspond with any of our conceptions.

Buddhism, according to the best informed Orientalists,
began by being 'pluralist' and ended, with the Mahâyâna,
by becoming 'monist'. It is not difficult to find texts
which, taken separately, support each of these two conceptions; but a text never represents more than the views
of its author. Ten contemporary texts may represent the
views of ten authors; it by no means necessarily follows
that no other opinions were current among the Buddhists
of their period. In the Orient there has always existed an
oral transmission, an 'unwritten literature', if I may

employ such an expression, whose influence is as great as, if not greater than that of the written works, and which represents a greater diversity of shades of opinion.

It is evident that we can base our investigations only on the actual documents which we possess, and these constitute only a small fraction of the Buddhist works which have existed and have been lost in the course of the centuries. As to the doctrines which were taught orally in these remote periods, they are wholly lost to us, and we have no right to affirm that there were among them some which differed from those which have come down to us in writing. In any case, a prolonged stay in Buddhist countries establishes the fact that in practice the differences between the Hinayâna and the Mahâyâna, and between the different sects of each, are not so clear-cut as they seem to be if one confines oneself to reading the treatises of the leaders of the Buddhist schools of philosophy. In practice, the various doctrines overlap and interlock at many points.

The present state of affairs leads us to suppose that a similar state existed in the past, and, with all necessary reservations, we may well believe that the germs of monism existed among the ancient pluralist Hinayânists, and that the monism of the Mahâyânists has never been absolute.

Several centuries before Christ Hinayâna Buddhism denied the existence of any spiritual matter or substance as the base and essence of phenomena, from which the latter arise, as, according to a Hindu comparison, 'the waves rise up from the ocean only to fall back into it'. The world, we are told, is constituted by the play of manifold forces. The elements which, by grouping themselves, give rise to the phenomena which we perceive, are devoid of any individual and lasting substance; we may picture them to ourselves as instantaneous discharges of energy. Whence do these forces arise? When and why did their activity commence? These are questions to which no reply is given; for such questions are regarded as exceeding the limits within which the human faculties can be successfully exercised. Learned Buddhists seem to have thought that the search for causes could be prolonged indefinitely, winning always more and more knowledge, but without ever reaching a final point where no further question could be asked.

According to this theory, the elements which constitute the things that we perceive do not endure even for the fraction of a second. The object which we contemplate, and which appears to us as a permanent entity—at least, during a longer or shorter lapse of time—is nothing but a continual succession of momentary events. According to the expression of many Orientalists, one of whom is Professor Stcherbatsky, for Buddhists the world is a *cinema*. The illusion of duration is produced, there as in the cinema, by the celerity with which these multiple events succeed one another.

Existence is movement and energy. That which does not act does not exist. One would, however, be wrong in conceiving this production as operating after a period of repose for the producing element. On the contrary, Buddhists hold that the element disappears immediately after it has arisen, the duration of its existence being comparable to that of a lightning flash. Its actual disappearance is the cause or the production of an effect. If there had been no disappearance there would have been no production, and so, just as it has been said that that which does not act does not exist, one may say that that which does not disappear does not exist.

It is on this theory of the momentary character of all formations (phenomena, beings, facts, whatever may be the name which we give them) that the chain of the Twelve Interdependent Origins is based, and especially the conception of existence as 'becoming', which forms part of it, as we saw in the chapter concerning the twelve origins.

If, following the advice of the Buddha, we wish to examine for ourselves the genuineness of the theory of instantaneousness, we are forced to recognize that we know the world only in the form of change, of appearances and disappearances.

Night ends when the day dawns, and the seasons follow one another with all the different aspects of nature which they bring with them. The internal dispositions and the external signs which constitute youth cease to exist when maturity arrives, and old age in its turn causes the disappearance of the signs that characterize the adult. The bud exists no longer when the flower is in bloom, and the flower has vanished when the fruit exists.

The verification of these well-marked changes is within the reach of all, but a more careful examination shows that the complete change, which alone impresses us, is brought about by a succession of changes which operate from one moment to the next. One does not become old suddenly; with the new-born child begins the process of appearances and disappearances which are incessantly changing it, physically and mentally, and which gradually lead to old age. It is the same for the bud, the flower, and the fruit, and for all other series of events.

Did the Buddha himself teach the instantaneousness of all elements and the plurality of original causes? No one can affirm this with certainty. It may suffice us to know that this doctrine was professed by Buddhists at a period relatively close to that in which he taught.

While attributing to the constitutive elements of all phenomena a period of existence so ephemeral that it might be considered as non-existent—their disappearance following immediately on their appearance—some Hina-yânists have allowed them, all the same, a kind of reality. A precarious reality, denied by those Buddhists who believed what a contemporary lama explained to me in a picturesque way: that 'each atom is a universe comprising myriads of beings and Buddhas, and that the law of production by interdependent origins (pratîtyasa-mûtpâda), which, in truth, is relativity and instanta-neousness, is at work in each one of the innumerable grains of sand that form the bed of the Ganges'.

And here we should pause, to note the very different meanings which are generally attached by Buddhists to the expressions 'to exist' and 'to be real'; expressions which the West, in current usage, employs almost as synonyms.

According to the Buddhists, the only thing that can be regarded as real is that which is self-engendered and homogeneous, that which is a 'self' whose existence does not depend on any external cause, which nothing has begotten, and which is not constituted by the grouping of various parts of different kinds.

Naturally, the being or thing that satisfies these conditions would also be eternal, for if it came into existence at a particular moment in time, this would mean that causes had *produced* it; similarly, if it disappeared at a particular moment in time, this fact would prove that its existence *depended on* certain conditions, and that these conditions having ceased, the existence of the being or the thing must also cease.

In short, for the Mahâyânists, and especially for those of Tibet, reality signifies 'self-existence', 'self-being'. This is why they deny the character of reality to the world which we perceive, for everywhere, and in everything, we see only objects which are produced by causes, depending on special conditions, and constituted by the unstable grouping of heterogeneous elements.

But when the Mahâyânists declare that a thing is not *real*, do they mean by that that the thing does not *exist*? By no means. The thing *exists*, no one denies it, but it has only a relative and dependent existence, and it contains not a single atom that possesses the character of *self-existence*. It is this fact which the disciples of Tsong Khapa have in mind when they state: 'The world exists, but it is not real.'

Yet another of the declarations already given calls for explanation. 'Each atom is an universe', we are told. The doctrine in question is especially prominent in certain Tibetan *damngags*.

The term *damngag* (*gtams ngag*) means counsel, advice, precept, but it has taken on the meaning of traditional teaching, of a secret doctrine orally transmitted from master to disciple. Most of the *damngags* consist in a mixture of doctrines belonging to different schools of Buddhist philosophy; sometimes they even include theories which appear to be mutually contradictory. The connection between disparate views, and agreement between opposed ideas, are effected by an original commentary incorporated in the *damngag*, borrowed, like the doctrines, from the ancient doctors of Buddhist philosophy.

The Tibetan *damngags* have no monopoly of the theories concerning the atoms. The school of Hindu philosophy (that is: non-Buddhist) known as Vaiseshika[1] taught that

[1] The date of the Vaiseshika-Sutras is extremely uncertain. They may already have existed in the first century after Christ; or it may be that they were not written down until the fifth or sixth century. Neither case excludes the possibility of the existence of the doctrine of the Vaiseshikas, and its oral transmission, before the period when it was expounded systematically in the sutras.

all objects are constituted of groups of atoms. According to the Vaiseshikas the atom is the most minute of the particles of matter; it is indivisible, eternal and invisible. Two or three of them must be grouped together for the mass thus formed to be perceptible. As for the groups of atoms, the Vaiseshikas regarded them as impermanent.

Those *damngags* which are concerned with atoms differ from the Vaiseshikas in that they do not fix a limit to the possibility of the division of the particles of matter; both a division continued to infinity and a limit to division are inconceivable, they say. In the same way, it is inadmissible that atoms, any more than anything else, can be eternal. The spiritual masters consider, however, that all speculations on this subject are vain and unprofitable.

What is taught by some of them is that all the objects which we perceive—a tree, a stone, an animal—are composed of atoms which are not at rest, but are moving and whirling round with dizzy rapidity. The Tibetan master illustrates, by the rapid and repeated snapping of the fingers, the fact that the composition of whatever group does not remain the same for two successive fractions of a second. Each snap of the fingers marks a change in the composition of the group.

How did the Tibetans, or those from whom they obtained these ideas, arrive at them?—Those who teach this doctrine believe that the masters who drew it up formulated the result of their own observations. But should we not rather believe that this was a case of

intuitive knowledge? Whatever the truth, I have met
those who stated that they *saw* the objects around them
as 'vortices' of particles which 'did not touch one
another', but 'danced opposite one another' or 'around
one another'.

Many among the Mahâyânists regard the world as
subjective, a mere projection of our minds. 'As the images
seen in dream, thus we should consider all aggregates' is
the precept of the *Prajñâ Pâramitâ*. And, the Buddhists
believe, of that which it is possible for us to perceive
and to know, there is nothing which is not 'formation',
'aggregate', 'group'.

In Tibet the learned adepts of the Dzogschen Sect
(sect of the 'Great Accomplishment') regard the world
as a pure mirage which we ourselves produce, and which
has no sort of existence outside ourselves. All that we
see, all that we feel, is identical with that which we see
and feel in our dreams, say the Dzogschenpas. In our
dreams we suffer, we are happy, we see ourselves living
in wealth or clad in rags; we meet all sorts of people,
we talk with them; passions arise in us, we love, we hate,
we perform various actions; and on waking all this
phantasmagoria disappears, often leaving us no memory
of it. But when we awake it is only one phase of the
dream that is finished; another phase—which we call
being awake—follows it, and we are still dreaming.

It is useless to attempt to disconcert a Dzogschenpa
scholar by saying that the fact that others see the same

things as ourselves is a proof of their reality. He has a reply ready. How can you prove, he would say, that other people exist? you are the only witness of their existence, and it is to yourself that you affirm that they exist. These people are no more than subjective images created by your own thoughts. If these 'other people' say that they see what you see, it is because you, yourself, are speaking through their mouths. They are like the people with whom you have talked in your dreams.

The Dzogschenpas did not invent this theory. It existed, long before them, in India and China. The celebrated Taoist philosopher Chuang Tzu gave picturesque expression to an analogous opinion in one of his works.

'Last night,' he wrote, 'I dreamt that I was a butterfly, and now I ask myself: Am I a man who dreamt that he was a butterfly, or am I a butterfly who is, for the moment, dreaming that he is a man?'

Is there any absolutely certain method of discovering the truth?

One is naturally tempted to invoke the evidence of memory, saying: 'I am sure that I am not a butterfly because I remember perfectly that yesterday I was a man, and that I have performed the actions proper to a man, and I remember the same thing in respect of last year, and for many years before that.'

To this argument, certain Tibetan lamas would reply as follows:

'Tell me, I beg you, *when* you *know* that you have performed such and such actions, or have witnessed such and such events at any period in the past?'

The question is a strange one, and likely to astonish the person questioned. However, after a moment's thought one is forced to admit that it is at the *present moment* that one is conscious of having performed such and such action, or witnessed such and such events. Then, after some necessary explanations, the lama will conclude that since it is at the *present moment* that you are conscious of these facts, the truth may be simply that *ideas* have *now* arisen in your mind. You have the *idea* that you have seen or done certain things, but only the *idea* exists.

No material proof will shake the opinion of these obstinate idealists. Tell them: 'As a proof that I have been a tailor, here is a coat which I have cut out and sewn. As proof that I have been an architect, here is a plan which I have drawn and a house which has been built according to this plan. As proof that I have been married, here is my son, aged twenty.'

Your imperturbable questioner will reply, smilingly: 'My friend, in your dreams you have often been a tailor, an architect, the father of a family, and all sorts of other individuals, and you have seen the results of their actions. All that, I repeat, is nothing but ideas projected by your mind, which is full of ideas. You yourself are nothing but an idea which exists, at this moment, in my mind. I have no infallible proof that you exist. I can only know that I have the idea, the sensation, that a man is before me and is speaking to me. This idea, this sensation, arises from a cause, but it is not absolutely certain that this cause is *really* the existence of a man who, I imagine, is arguing with me.'

A dream, like any other phenomenon, must actually have a cause: Buddhism is the Doctrine of Causality. The causes specified, here, are ignorance and the 'interdependent origins', which are both engendered by ignorance and engender it. In this case *pratîtyasamûtpâda* (interdependent origins) should be accepted according to its meaning in the Mahâyâna, i.e. as the general law of the production, interdependently, of all the elements which constitute the world.

Again, it is said that what gives rise to the mirage of the world is the false distinction that imagines differences in identity, endows that which it has arbitrarily separated with a special name and special qualities, and imagines it as performing special actions. The adepts of the Zen Sect are strongly urged to liberate themselves from this tendency to false discrimination, in order to attain to the perception of 'identity'. Even more plainly, the *Prajñâ Pâramitâ* gives us the wise advice not to abandon ourselves to our imagination, this being regarded as the creator of manifold illusions, and of the great illusion, the mirage of the world.

Various words employed in the Mahâyâna have often been interpreted by foreigners as meaning the Absolute, Reality, the First Principle from which all things originate, or even, as some have thought, a God, or the Buddha considered as God. These interpretations differ widely from those of the Buddhists.

*Âlayâ vijñâna* (store of consciousness) represents, for Mahâyânists, a sort of accumulated treasury in which are the subtle forces produced by all the thoughts and all the actions which have ever been thought or performed; and when the Buddhists who admit the existence of this *âlayâ vijñâna* say that this 'store' contains also the seeds which will produce thoughts and acts in the future, it is because they hold that these seeds *are* the thoughts and actions of the past.

The Tibetans have a special word, *kunji*, which means the 'base of all things'. This is clearly not a literal translation of 'store of consciousness', yet Orientalists usually consider *kunji* as the Tibetan equivalent of *âlayâ vijñâna*.

It appears from the explanations which I have obtained from learned Tibetans that *kunji* means the mind, this being the 'base' of the imaginary ideas which create the mirage of the world. We find again in the Tibetan *damngags* (the orally transmitted body of traditional and esoteric doctrines) the above-mentioned Mahâyânist conceptions. There it is said that the innumerable moments of consciousness, the mental representations, the infinite number of ideas which have existed—without its being possible to perceive any origin or beginning of this activity—constitute the 'base' (kunji) whence they emanate afresh as causes of all the moments of consciousness, of all the sensations, perceptions, of all the phenomena that arise.

Force continually emanates from this 'base' or 'store', and force is continually stored up therein. This 'base' or 'store', however, is situated nowhere outside the world. It is the *samsâra* (korwa, in Tibetan); the 'round' as it is conceived by Lamaist initiates.

This 'round' revolves by the effect of mental activity, which releases physical energy, and at the same time depends on this latter for its upkeep.

In these doctrines, *kunji nampar shespa* becomes the fundamental consciousness or the 'consciousness-basis of everything', and is often identified with *lo* (blo), the mind envisaged as a collection of mental operations which repeat themselves by force of habit. This theory is not peculiar to the Tibetan schools of philosophy. The Lankavâtara sûtra insists upon it strongly in its declaration that the world is *vâsânâ*. *Vâsânâ* means 'memory'. When this term is used in connection with man and man's doings it is especially understood as the knowledge—generally the dim knowledge—or the propensities derived from the memory stored in the 'subconscious', which is the result of the impressions caused by past actions. It differs from the intellectual, reasoned memory, and leads to the instinctive repetition of physical or mental acts which have been accomplished in the past. Consequently *vâsânâ* has been translated as 'habit-energy'.

Besides this restricted meaning, *vâsânâ* has other meanings. The 'habit-energy' is closely related to the collective *Karman*, and in another way it is also said to be related to physics as playing a part in the succession of phenomena.

The detection of the working of this 'habit-energy' and the liberation from its bonds is considered to be *Nirvâna*.

Another term used by the Mahâyânists is *Dharma kâya*, to which they give various meanings. Some see it as the impersonal spiritual source from which emanate the Buddhas who appear in our world—such as the historical Gautama, and his supposed predecessors and successors —or the Buddhas who appear in whatsoever other worlds. For this reason, these are called 'apparitional bodies' (nirmâna kâya). However, there exist Buddhists who believe that just as the Buddhists who appear in the various worlds are generated by the *Dharma kâya*, these Buddhas also contribute to sustain the Dharma kâya, which is but the sum of their spiritual energy.

According to another view, *Dharma kâya* is the 'Body of the Dharmas' (dharmas = constituent elements) and is thus the totality of the world. Yet, we must beware of taking this 'totality of the world' as meaning the Absolute, for to the Buddhists the world is neither the Absolute nor the Reality. These, as has already been explained, are declared to be indescribable and inconceivable. Moreover, some Mahâyânist Schools distinguish two aspects of Dharma kâya: the aspect 'substance', which is said to be permanent, and the aspect 'knowledge', which is said to be impermanent.

I have heard Tibetan scholars declare that *Dharma kâya* is 'in' *kunji*. As they took *kunji* (the basis of all) to be the mind, their declaration was tantamount to saying that the concept of *Dharma kâya*, and all theories about it, concerned relativity, and were not to be taken as expressing the Reality.

Again, another term found in the Mahâyânist Scriptures is *Tathata*. Nowadays it is specially in favour in the Japanese Zen sect. *Tathata* means 'identity', 'suchness'; and this identity is recognized, according to the Zenists, when the mind ceases to make arbitrary distinctions.

These terms and others have been studied, in all their various meanings, in the attempt to discover by this means the various conceptions of the Absolute which have been held by the Buddhists. This is a useless search. Although they were warned by their Master against the uselessness of metaphysical speculations, the Buddhists could not entirely resist their racial tendencies; they have elaborated numerous theories concerning matter, mind, and phenomena, although they have never allowed themselves to be tempted to describe the Absolute, Reality.

The Reality, they think, excludes both duality and non-duality; it cannot be expressed in words any more than it can be imagined. All Buddhists recognize that whatever knowledge we are able to acquire is limited and conditioned by our powers of perception. All our knowledge is relative, and all the objects attained by our knowledge are, consequently, also relative. The Absolute is the Unknowable; if known it would become relative.

The word 'Void' (sûnya) which we find in the

Mahâyânist texts is generally used there to indicate the absence of all that our mind could conceive while operating within the limits of relativity. The Void, among Buddhists, has never the meaning of absolute nothingness which Westerners have sometimes wished to give it. On the one hand, it indicates the lack of any autogenous and individual substance in all the constituent elements of phenomena, their interdependence, and their relative character, and, on the other hand, it is a name for the Reality, the Absolute, which is inaccessible, being beyond the limits accessible to our powers of perception.

We are thus, after many deviations, brought back to the wise counsels of the Buddha:

'Do not think: the world is eternal; it is not eternal; it is infinite, it is limited.

'The world is accustomed to cling to a duality; everything is, or nothing is; but for him who perceives, in truth and in wisdom, how things are produced and perish in the world, for him there is neither being nor non-being.' (Samyutta Nikâya.)

ETHICS

Having acquired Right Views—or, at least, having rejected the most erroneous views—having learnt the habit of scrutinizing the motives of his actions, and discerning their probable effect, the disciple has become capable of regulating his conduct in a better manner, better for himself and for others.

Here, especially, occurs the distinction between the

two 'paths', the path of those who remain 'in the world' and the path of the *aryas*: i.e. of the noble disciples who have lifted themselves above the routine life of men absorbed in the affairs of the world.

The *arya*, especially according to the Tibetan conception, which on this point is analogous to that of the Hindus, is not governed by any rigid moral code. He *knows* how he should act, according to the circumstances in which his act is to be accomplished, so that the result of this latter may be useful, so that it may suppress suffering and ignorance, so that it may produce happiness and edification.

This Way of complete liberty, on which one walks with no other guide than one's own knowledge, is evidently perilous, and the spiritual masters of India, like those of Tibet, have never failed to warn their disciples against its dangers. Over-confidence is disastrous, and it is picturesquely said that he who uses his liberty to give rein to his passions, instead of using it to work more effectively for the good of others, and towards his own improvement, becomes a demon.

Rules have, therefore, been laid down for the unlearned, whether members of the religious order or laymen.

The first few of these rules, like all moral laws in the world, are of a purely social character, and not especially remarkable. No matter to what religion one belongs, no matter what philosophy one believes, or even if one is completely agnostic, the fact that one is a member of a group of human beings obliges one to observe these rules, in order that the members of this group can live in safety.

These are the 'Five Precepts' enjoined on all Buddhists:

> Not to kill.
> Not to take that which has not been given to you.
> Not to indulge in illicit sexual relations.
> Not to lie.
> Not to drink intoxicating liquors.

In addition to the above, the following five 'precepts' should be observed by members of the religious Order:

> Not to eat or drink outside the permitted times.
> Not to dance, sing, or go to entertainments or to theatres.
> Not to adorn the body with flowers, scents, or unguents.
> Not to use high or wide beds or seats.
> Not to receive either gold or silver.

The third precept, which enjoins the layman to abstain from illicit sexual relations, is, for members of the Order, replaced by the injunction to preserve complete chastity.

These same 'precepts' are laid down in a more developed form, and are then called the 'Ten Meritorious Actions' (meritorious in the sense that their results are beneficial).

To abstain from killing is good.
To abstain from theft is good.
To abstain from illicit sexual relations is good.
To abstain from lying is good.
To abstain from evil-speaking is good.
To abstain from hard and hurtful words is good.
To abstain from covetousness is good.
To abstain from cruelty is good.
To understand correctly is good. (Majjhima Nikâya.)

There is also a list of the ten 'non-meritorious actions', which reproduces the above list in the opposite sense: 'To kill is evil', 'To steal is evil', and so on.

And here is a contemporary paraphrase of the ten precepts, based on the commandments found in the sermons attributed to the Buddha:

'Not to kill, to have regard for all life, human, animal, or vegetable, not to destroy carelessly.

'Not to purloin or steal. To help everyone to possess the fruits of his labour.

'Not to commit adultery. To live chastely.

'Not to lie. To speak the truth with discretion, not to harm another, but with good-will, charity, and wisdom.

'Not to use fermented drinks, nor any stupefying drugs.

'Not to swear. Not to indulge in frivolous, unclean, or harmful conversation. To speak with restraint and dignity when one has a reason for speech; otherwise to keep silent.

'Not to slander or disparage; not to repeat slanders or

calumnies. Not to criticize and blame, but to search for the good points in our neighbour, so that we may sincerely defend those who are attacked.

'Not to covet jealously the advantages enjoyed by those around us. To rejoice in the happiness which comes to them.

'To reject unkindness, anger, scorn, ill-will. Not to foster hatred, even against those who have harmed us. To entertain, toward all living beings, feelings of kindness, good-will, and love.

'To fight ignorance in and around oneself. To be vigilant in the search for truth, and in the dread of falling into passive acceptance of doubt, or into indifference, or into error leading away from the Path to peace.'

Although this programme of virtuous conduct, according to the Buddhist conception, is clear in itself, a few additional details as to the various interpretations which are given to it may be of interest.

The injunction not to kill is not understood by Buddhists in the same way as by Jews and Christians, who both find their authority in the Decalogue of Moses. These allow so many exceptions to this commandment that it becomes, in effect, non-existent. In the first place, according to them, the prohibition only applies to men, so that it is allowable to kill animals for food, or even simply for pleasure, as in hunting the fox, etc., where one kills animals which one does not eat. The death-penalty inflicted on criminals also seems to them quite legitimate. It does not occur to them that their act is more odious than that of the assassin himself, for he may have been driven to the crime by reasons by which they are not moved, or that, in any case, the man who has killed unlawfully has risked his life in so doing, while those who cause him to be legally assassinated run no risk whatever, which stains their action with a certain cowardice. Further, the execution of a criminal is accompanied by basely vindictive sentiments and by a sadistic cruelty for which there is no excuse. If one considers that a man is a permanent danger to others, and one believes—which is very arguable—that it is not enough to incarcerate him for life as is done to dangerous madmen, so as to prevent him from doing any harm, one might, at least, suppress him without his knowledge, by methods which would spare him the prolonged agony of waiting for execution, which is carried out while he is fully conscious.

The precautions taken to prevent a man condemned to death from committing suicide, and the fact that we try to cure him if he falls ill, and do everything possible to prevent him from dying, so as to have the satisfaction of killing him when he is cured, are aberrations which in future ages will be viewed with the same horror with which we now regard the torture-chambers of the Middle Ages.

Apart from the execution of criminals, murder is still considered legitimate in war, and also when a man is himself threatened and in danger of being killed. It is difficult to deny that a man who lives in association with other men, and who enjoys the advantages which result from their collaboration, is in duty bound to defend this society if it is attacked—but it is necessary that this society should have been of *real* advantage to him. As to the defence of one's own person, anyone who is neither a saint nor a sage has the right to protect his own life.

Where new aberrations are appearing in the West is in the excuses made for so-called 'crimes of passion'. An assassin who was animated by the desire to appropriate money may, perhaps, if he finds himself in comfortable circumstances, become an 'honest man', but the *crime passionel* reveals, in the man who commits it, the existence of pernicious tendencies which are liable to blaze up at any moment and to lead to new crimes. He is a madman of the most dangerous kind, who should never be taken before a tribunal, but should be interned for life in a lunatic asylum immediately after his crime.

The ideas which I have just expressed are not new, and I do not pretend to be their author; I only wish, in recalling them to the reader's memory, to show the great difference which exists between the Semitic interpretation, Jewish or Christian, of the command not to kill, and that of the Buddhists.

All Buddhists unanimously admit that the prescription is formal: one should not kill, one should kill *nothing*, neither human beings nor animals; one should *never* kill, under whatever circumstances, no matter what risks one runs, or what causes incite one to murder.

This is not an arbitrary commandment; it derives from reasons which are considered convincing by Buddhists. Laymen can judge, by their own love of life, how much others are attached to it, and as one is not really a Buddhist unless one has a compassionate heart, lay disciples regard with horror the act of inflicting on another the physical and mental suffering which is involved in the loss of life.

As to those, either members of the religious Order or lay disciples, who follow the superior Path 'out of the world', the spiritual light which they have acquired has produced in them such a detachment from life and its interests, such a profound pity for the beings possessed by the thirst for existence and happiness, that far from thinking of destroying them, they would allow themselves to be stripped and killed without resistance. The legend of the young prince who gave himself as food to a tigress is an example of this attitude.[1]

Such is the Buddhist ideal. It is uplifted far above our utilitarian considerations; it arises, as we have seen, from a conception of the world and of the nature of our self which is totally different from that which is current in the West.

However, when a doctrine numbers several hundreds of millions of nominal followers, it is inevitable that the great majority of these should be very imperfectly penetrated by its philosophical principles and the virtues which proceed from them.

[1] See page 116.

Among the Buddhists there are some who have found specious arguments to justify the eating of meat.

In the first place, there is the story of the Buddha whose last meal, according to some, was a dish of boar's flesh offered to him by a smith in whose house he ate the repast. This indigestible food, eaten when he was already suffering from dysentery, made his condition worse, and caused his death at the age of eighty-one years.

Since we have been duly warned by the Buddha himself that his doctrine did not derive its value from the fact that it was preached by him, and that nothing but its agreement with the real facts should incline us to accept it, after having examined it minutely, it is quite indifferent whether the Buddha did, or did not, eat meat. For some time I accepted the idea that the dinner at which Chunda, the smith, offered boar's meat to the Buddha might be historically true, but since then several sojourns in India have changed my opinion on this point. Those Buddhists who state that the term 'boar's delight' which figures in the texts refers to a kind of fungus of which boars are very fond seem to me to be right. The Buddha did not belong to that class of Tantric ascetics who habitually violate all established rules as to the purity of food, and whom one may sometimes see beside a sewer, eating the filth carried away by it. This kind of 'saint' arose only after the epoch in which he lived, and in any case, even if there did then exist a few examples of such ascetics, neither the Buddha, nor his masters, nor his own disciples, had anything in common with them. But in India respectable ascetics have never eaten meat, and no one thinks of offering it to them.

Moreover, we read in the canonical texts (Maha-Parinibbana Sutta) that the Buddha forbade those of his disciples who dined with him in the house of the smith to eat this harmful dish, saying that it was unfit for aliment, and ordering it to be buried; which might very well refer to poisonous fungi, or, as Professor Narasu suggested, to the root of a bulbous plant named *sukara kanda*,[1] which is eatable, but for which the root of a poisonous plant might have been substituted, or been mingled with it by mistake.

However this may be, members of the Buddhist Order have so thoroughly accepted the precept 'not to kill' as applying to all beings, human as well as animal, that one of the articles of their monastic outfit is a filter, through which they have to pass their drinking-water, so as to avoid swallowing, and thereby killing, the microscopic animals contained in the water.

This noble zeal often weakens in respect of the vegetarian diet. It is practically only among the Chinese Buddhists that all, laymen as well as members of the Order, are strictly faithful to it.

In Tibet, climatic conditions and the difficulty of obtaining vegetables at high altitudes make the vegetarian régime far from easy. All Tibetans are fond of meat, but

[1] The expression used in the canonical texts is: *sukara maddava*, which some interpret as 'a delicious morsel of boar', and others, as has been explained, as 'boar's delight'.

only rich people living in the towns eat it every day. The peasants, and even the herdsmen living among their cattle, eat it but rarely; I was able to realize this during the long years which I spent among them. There are many lamas who, on principle, entirely abstain from animal food. But whether they eat meat or not, all Tibetans—save a few magicians, followers of Tantric doctrines—declare that meat-eating is an evil action which brings harmful results on him who is guilty of it, and creates a deleterious psychic atmosphere in places where it is habitually committed.

I have, however, heard lama-magicians and hermits express some original opinions on this subject.

'Most men,' one of them said to me, 'eat like animals, to satisfy their hunger, without thinking of the action which they are performing and of its results. These ignorant persons do well to abstain from meat and fish. Others, on the other hand, are well aware of what becomes of the material elements which they swallow when they eat an animal. They know that their assimilation brings with it other psychic elements, which are joined to them. He who has acquired this knowledge may, at his own risk, enter into such associations, and endeavour to draw from them results useful to the victim of the sacrifice. The question is, how to know whether the elements of animal origin which he swallows will give renewed strength to the animal instincts already existing in him, or whether he will be capable of transmuting into intelligent and spiritual forces the substance which comes to him from the animal, and which will be reborn in him in the form of his own activity.'[1]

There are several passages in the Pâli Suttas which Buddhists might possibly cite as authority for eating meat without fear of breaking the first precept.

We read, in the Amaghandha Sutta of the Sutta Nipâta:

'It is not the eating of meat which renders one impure, but being brutal, hard, slanderous, pitiless, miserly.

'That which renders one impure is not the eating of meat, it is hatred, intemperance, obstinacy, bigotry, deceit, envy, pride, presumption, indulgence towards those who are guilty of injustice.'

It does not seem, however, that the *bhikkhus* (members of the Order) of the southern Buddhist countries seek in such passages an excuse for their greed as far as meat is concerned. Such declarations, like many others of a similar nature, were directed against the Phariseeism of the Brahmins, who boasted of a purity which consisted only in external acts and ritual practices. Such passages are numerous in the Pâli scriptures.

'It is not the shaven head which makes a *sramana* (ascetic) of the man who neglects his duties and who lies. If one is wholly eaten up with covetousness and desire, how should one be a *sramana*?'

'One is not a *bhikkhu* (religious mendicant) because one

[1] See my books: *Magic and Mystery in Tibet* (Kendall, New York); *With Mystics and Magicians in Tibet* (John Lane, London).

begs from others. It is because one has concentrated the whole doctrine in oneself that one is a *bhikkhu*.' (Dhammapada.)

In the same way, it is said that it is not because one remains continually silent or because one admits no woman to one's bed that one is an *arhat* (the highest degree of spiritual elevation); one is an *arhat* if one is full of compassion for all beings, if one acts after due reflection, etc.

No Buddhist of the South has ever concluded from this that the *bhikkhu* ought not to cut his hair, that he ought not to beg his food, or that it was allowable for him to take a wife.

In order to justify their conduct, the *bhikkhus* of Ceylon, Burma, and other countries of southern Asia quote a saying which they attribute to the Buddha, and which, if it is authentic, is a somewhat ironical sally. According to this, members of the Order are allowed— and still more laymen—to eat meat when they have not themselves killed the animal, when they have not ordered it to be killed by another person, when the animal has not been killed especially for their consumption, or, as some of them say: 'when one does not *know* that it has been killed'; that is to say, when one was not warned that it was going to be killed. Happy ignorance, most willingly cultivated, which enables these casuists to satisfy their culpable greed, thereby setting a deplorable example! I hasten to add, however, that there are honourable exceptions among the *bhikkhus*; in the Sagain mountains, in Burma, I have known whole communities of *bhikkhus* who were strictly vegetarian, and there were many pious laymen who imitated them.

In Tibet, where, as I have already said, sinners do not seek to excuse their sin, it is usual to abstain from meat on the days of Buddhist observances, three times a month; on the day of the new moon, on the last day of the month, and, especially, on the fifteenth of the month.[1]

The lamas and a great many laymen eat no meat during the whole of the first month of the year, and during this month it is strictly forbidden to slaughter animals. This prohibition also extends, each month, to the above-mentioned dates.

I have not spoken of the abstention from fish, for the Tibetans do not eat it, except in the districts which border on China, where the example of the Chinese has made them overcome the repugnance which this food inspires in them.

In connection with the first precept, of course, the conduct of a Buddhist in time of war has to be considered. Ought he to fight? Opinions are divided. If one puts this question to Japanese followers of the Zen Sect, they will unhesitatingly answer that one must fight for one's country. In fact, the élite of the samurai belonged to this sect.

[1] These are lunar months, and the first two dates are, respectively, the eighth and the thirtieth.

It is said that Toki-mune (1264-1283), the shogun who defeated the fleet of Kublai Khan when it attempted to conquer Japan, was a zealous follower of the Zen Sect. On two occasions he caused the envoys of the Khan, who demanded the submission of Japan, to be decapitated. Then, when the enemy approached, he went to his spiritual master, Tsu Yuen, in order to receive his final instructions.—'Revered Master,' he said to him, 'an imminent danger threatens the country.'—'How will you face it?' asked Tsu Yuen. For sole response, Toki-mune gave one of those sharp exclamations which are habitual to Zenists.—'Oh, the roar of the lion?' said Tsu Yuen. 'Thou art a real lion. Go, and never turn thy back on the enemy!' Toki-mune gained the victory.

In Japan's feudal period it was not rare for two opposing generals, both Zenists, on meeting during a battle, to exchange blows and stoic phrases inspired by the teaching of their spiritual masters; as did Shin-gen and Ken-shin. The national hero, Masa-shige, who committed suicide with his officers after a defeat, and General Nogi, who conquered Port Arthur, and who, with his wife, committed suicide to show his fidelity to the Emperor at the time of the ruler's funeral, excite the enthusiasm of certain Zenists . . . perhaps of all, although Zen is not lacking in other ideals more in accordance with the spirit of Buddhism.

At the opposite extreme to this warlike 'Buddhism' we find a Buddhism that exalts absolute non-resistance.

According to a tradition, of which the basis is almost certainly historically true, the family of the Buddha, and the whole of the Sakya clan to which he belonged, perished as victims of their inviolable respect for the lives of others.

Threatened by a neighbouring chief, they undertook the solemn engagement not to kill in their own defence, and they even refused to receive among them one of their family who, being absent at the time when this engagement was made, had killed some of the enemy. They all allowed themselves to be massacred without attempting to defend themselves.

The narratives of this drama say that rivers of blood ran in the town, and that the Buddha, then an old man, one day seated himself at the edge of a well into which his relatives had been thrown.

Those who believe—or who know—that actions of this kind send forth into the world forces tending to check violence, will attach an inestimable value to the sacrifice of the Sakyas, but the majority of Buddhists could not refrain from according to the Sakyas themselves a personal and material reward for their fidelity to the precept 'not to kill.' These heroes of detachment and charity are, according to these good people, reborn among the gods.

The rule generally admitted, in respect of personal defence, is that a Buddhist ought not to kill, even to save his life, and certainly the breaker of this rule has no right to the name of Buddhist. As to whether it is allowable to kill in order to defend another person, and more especially to defend those who have a right to our protection—wife and children, parents, servants, travelling companions—the question is debatable. It seems, however, that the attitude which is most generally approved is that of defence, while endeavouring, as far as possible, to render the aggressor harmless without taking his life.

This question brings us back to the problem of what a Buddhist ought to do in time of war. The answers which I have received, on this point, differ widely. Complete abstention, say some; one should let oneself be shot by the military authorities rather than kill. Others reply: one should never enlist as a soldier, and if one is forced to form part of an army, one should undertake the hardest work, the most dangerous tasks, and hold one's life cheap, but never kill. And others, again, have answered that in refusing to kill the enemy one increases the risks run by the fighting men of one's own country. Every enemy whom one does not put out of action when one has the chance of doing so may cause the death of several of one's compatriots, or of one's relations.

Is there, in reality, any object in such discussions among Buddhists? Yes, if, as has happened, Buddhism serves as a 'religion' for a large body of followers, and if, in consequence, its doctrine has been brought down to their level. No, if Buddhism remains what the Buddha desired that it should be: a search for knowledge by philosophically minded men, already largely detached from the passions and interests that agitate the world.

The second precept: 'Not to take that which has not been given', which is to be understood in the sense of 'freely given', applies to numerous cases, many of which concern social relations. The definition of theft leads to the definition of legitimate property. There are not wanting Buddhists who consider that the simple fact of possessing a thing does not necessarily imply that one has any moral right to possess it.

In the time of the Buddha, Hindu society settled in its own way, or rather, ignored the mass of problems which we call 'social'. The poor were numerous, as they still are in the East, but then, as today, no one was in danger of death from starvation, save during periods of famine. Poverty in the form in which it exists in the West today had not yet been created, and the relations between capital and labour gave rise to no complications.

In this simple-mannered society theft was not disguised by any artifice, but was merely the act of taking something 'which was not given'. The old formula, however, lent itself to all the developments which might be required of it, in the future, in societies whose life was to become more complicated.

As to the third precept, abstention from illicit sexual relations, it should be noted that this prohibition is of a social order. There is no such thing as a Buddhist rite destined to consecrate, religiously, the union of two

consorts. These make their union legal by satisfying the
formalities customary in their respective countries. Nor
does Buddhism lay down any rules as to the forms of
marriage. Monogamy, polygamy, and polyandry all
exist among Buddhists. These are matters which concern
only civil society and the private convenience of the
individual; they have nothing to do with the philosophical doctrines or the aim of Buddhism. Whether a
man has one wife or whether he has several, whether a
woman has one husband or several husbands, as happens
in Tibet, the only thing that matters is that they should
act loyally toward one another, that they should show
kindness and devotion toward their consorts and their
children.

By illicit sexual relations is meant adultery and the
seduction of young girls living under the protection of
their family.

The reciprocal duties of marriage are laid down as
follows in the *Sigâlovâda Sutta* of the *Dighâ Nikâya*:

The husband should love his wife—
    By treating her with respect.
    By treating her with kindness.
    By being faithful to her.
    By causing her to be honoured by others.
    By giving her suitable ornaments and clothes.

The wife should show her affection for her husband—
    By ordering her household aright.

By being hospitable to kinsmen and friends of her
   husband.
By being a chaste wife.
By being a thrifty housekeeper.
By showing skill and diligence in all she has to do.

This table shows us a clear division between the duties
of the two spouses, according to ancient custom, but
there is no sign that one of them should be sacrificed to
the other. It is worth remarking, also, that in contrast
to the religious and civil codes of the West, there is no
question here of obedience or of the subjection of the
wife to her husband.

If Buddhism rigorously condemns debauchery and lust,
it in no way glorifies continence for its own sake. Complete chastity, which is demanded of members of the
Order, appears to be, in their case, a consequence of their
detachment from physical sensations and the concentration
of their mind on spiritual aims. This attitude is calculated
to reduce the passions to silence, whether in the case of
sensual appetites, or the thirst for riches, or ambition for
power and glory. One may recall, here, what was said
in Chapter I of the renunciation of the *sannyâsins*: they
reject that which they have ceased to desire, or which
even inspires them with repulsion.

Buddhism has never taught that the mere fact of remaining strictly celibate could lead the disciple to knowledge. No doubt it may give to him (or her) greater
independence, by liberating him from moral ties and

material burdens, and in thus rendering easier of attainment peace of mind, impartiality of opinion, and the freedom of judgement and action necessary to him who aspires to Wisdom; but neither chastity, nor voluntary poverty, nor any other ascetic practice can give intelligence to the stupid, or knowledge to the ignorant.

Under the same heading as untruths are forbidden all 'verbal actions', as they are technically named, which might harm others or cause them pain in any way. The Tibetan masters insist also that one should use discretion in applying this precept; that obedience to it should serve to benefit other beings, and should not become for them a cause of suffering.

It goes without saying that a man questioned by the brigands who have captured him should not, under pretext of telling the truth, inform them that he has a travelling companion, and that this latter is hidden in such and such a place, or has fled in such and such a direction. It seems absurd to mention this, but one meets people who declare that the truth ought to be respected for its own sake, and that in all cases the truth must be told, no matter what catastrophes may result from the telling.

The prohibition of stupefying drinks and the use of drugs having any influence on the mind is strict, and easily explained. The pursuit of knowledge by means of attention, observation, analysis, and reflection, demands clearness of mind; consequently all that may produce a more or less pronounced derangement of the mental functions, may diminish acuteness of perception, and may produce a morbid excitement of the senses and the mind, or deaden them, is above all things to be avoided.

The Tibetans, who are not lacking in humour, illustrate the importance of abstaining from alcoholic drinks by an amusing anecdote.

A member of the Order found himself compelled by a demon to disobey the Buddhist precepts, by committing, at his own choice, one of the three following actions: to kill a goat, to have sexual relations with a woman, or to drink alcohol.

Having thought it over, the poor man concluded that assuredly the least of these faults would be to drink the forbidden liquor. He did so, and when he was drunk lust arose in him; he lay with the woman, and then, to please his mistress by giving her a good meal, he killed the goat.

Buddhists are also enjoined to earn their living by means which can neither directly nor indirectly cause suffering to others.

Four kinds of commerce are forbidden to them: (1) Selling or manufacturing arms. (2) Dealing in living beings; not only the slave trade, but also the sale of animals. If, for a good reason, the master of an animal cannot keep it, he should endeavour to find for it a new master who will treat it kindly.

A Buddhist may use animals to help him in his work, but he must consider them as beings endowed with feelings, and never as objects to be bought and sold for money, as though they were inanimate things. (3) Dealing in meat. (4) Dealing in intoxicants; drugs being included, and poisons. This last term does not apply to poisons used in medicinal preparations.

In the permissible ways of earning his livelihood the Buddhist must of course abstain from actions which have been condemned by the other precepts. He should be an honest business man, a conscientious worker or servant, a teacher who has at heart the progress of his pupils, and so on.

The *Sijalovada Sutta*, a translation of which will be found in the Appendix, will give the reader some idea of the moral code which was held in honour among the lay Buddhists of old.

# VI

## KARMAN[1]

THE doctrine of *Karman*, which is simply that of Causality, is common to all Hindu philosophies. Before the time of the Buddha it had already been the subject of long and subtle controversies among the Brahmins, and each of the philosophical systems of Indian origin has elaborated special theories on the subject of Karman, its nature and its working.

It seems that there was a time in which the doctrine of Karman formed part of an esoteric teaching. It was then probably opposed to the popular beliefs which attributed the important events that occurred in the world to the will of the gods, as also the minor happenings which concerned each individual. A man was born deaf, blind, weak, or strong and without physical defects because a god had been pleased to produce such a being. Again, prosperity or poverty, success or failure, fortunate or unfortunate incidents, and in fact, all the aspects of the life of the individual, depended on the will of the gods. The reasons on which this will was grounded, or which caused it, remained mysterious and inexplicable;

[1] Foreign authors generally write 'Karma'. I have retained the neutral form Karman, which is more generally employed in the East.

at the same time, it was neither absolute nor unchangeable. The god might be won over by adoration, by signs of respect, by offerings; hence the ceremonies, rites, and clergy needed for their celebration. In short, these good people believed that there existed means to induce a change of mind in the god who wished them ill, and to awake the desire of benevolence in the mind of a god who was indifferent. In all ages and in all civilizations the mass of mankind has thought in this manner, and such dealings with the Divinity form the effective part of all religions.

It was so in India, then, before the time of the Buddha. But among the thinkers doubts arose. They asked themselves whether the facts of which they were the witnesses were, in reality, the results of an arbitrary will arising *without a cause*. This seemed inadmissible. The will, the manifestation of desire, must be produced by something, and consequently, if it has a cause, this cause itself must have one. . . . A door was thus opened on the infinite.

In an oft-quoted passage of the *Brahmana of the Hundred Paths* we find confirmation of the esoteric character of the doctrine of Karman among the ancient Brahmins. As constantly happens in discussions among Orientals, the answer given to the question propounded in the dialogue which has come down to us seems to be irrelevant. We shall see presently, however, that it ignores, perhaps expressly, the ideas on which the question is based, because these, in the opinion of the respondent, are incorrect, so that he substitutes another view for them.

Artabhâga asks the renowned sage Yâjnavalkya: "When a man dies, his voice goes into the fire, his breath into the wind, his eye to the sun, his thought to the moon, his ear to the heavens, his body to the earth, his ego to the ether, the hair of his body and his head to the plants and the trees; his blood and his seed flow into the waters. But where, then, dwells the man himself?'

Yâjnavalkya, to this very direct question, answers: 'Artabhâga, this knowledge is for us two alone. Not a word on this subject to the people.' And Yâjnavalkya 'having taken Artabhâga by the hand, the two of them drew aside and talked together. And they spoke of actions (Karman); by pure acts man becomes pure, by evil acts he becomes evil.'

This secret knowledge, the possession of an élite of thinkers,which they were disinclined to proclaim openly, Buddhism proceeded to make the basis of its teaching, proclaiming: *Ye dharmâ hetuprabhavâ*: All things spring from a cause.

This apparently simple formula gives rise, when one studies it, to numerous complications. But before proceeding to a summary description of some of the aspects of Karman, let me say that the Buddhist multitude hardly considers this latter save under the form of moral retribution. The desire for justice which is instinctive in the great majority of men has made them imagine, as the causes of the evils which afflict them or others, evil actions which have been committed either in this life or in a previous life by the person who is now suffering. According to this artless conception, good deeds, on the contrary, must necessarily lead to happiness, either in this life or in a future life, for the man who has performed them.

This conception of automatic and impersonal justice appears, to most Buddhists, infinitely superior to that which attributes to the arbitrary will of a god the misery or happiness of the beings who are in that case merely his playthings.

In fact, according to this theory, no one is wronged. If we are born healthy in mind and body, in circumstances favouring a happy future, it is because we ourselves have produced, in previous lives, the causes which have brought about our birth in these conditions. On the other hand, cruelty, avarice, sensuality, intemperance, and other vices, if unrestrained during our previous lives, will ensure a birth under unfavourable conditions.

A work which enjoys great popularity among Hinayânist Buddhists is *The Questions of King Milinda*,[1] in which we read as follows:

'The king asked Nâgasêna: Why are not men all alike? Why are some of them short-lived and others long-lived? Why are some ugly and others handsome?

[1] The king here called Milinda is a historical personage, one of the Greek kings who reigned over Bactria, to the east of India, after the conquests of Alexander the Great, 200 B.C. His name was Menandrosa or Menandrou.

Why are some powerful, others rich, others poor? Why are some born in lowly social conditions and others among the upper classes? Why are some stupid and others intelligent?

'Nâgasêna answered: Why are not all plants the same? Why have some a sour taste while others are salt, or bitter, or acid, or astringent, or sweet to the taste?

'It seems to me, said the king, that these differences come from the difference in the quality of the seeds.

'Thus it is, O king, with the differences that you have noticed among men, the reason for which you asked me. All beings have each their own Karman; they are the heirs of their Karman. They have their Karman for ancestor, for family, and for supreme Lord. It is Karman that classifies them in all sorts of categories.'

And elsewhere:

'My deeds (Karman) are my riches, my deeds are my inheritance, my deeds are the womb which bore me. My deeds are the race to which I belong, my deeds are my refuge.' (Anguttara Nikâya.)

We will return to these statements, and examine the explanations which have been given of them.

Having been born under conditions determined by his past deeds, it is for the man to overcome the difficulties caused by his mistakes, and to prepare better conditions for his present life and his future lives. In the same way it is important that he who is enjoying a happiness which he owes to his virtuous conduct in the past should beware of committing evil deeds that will involve him in suffering in the near, or distant, future.

Pious and simple people have embroidered on this theme *ad infinitum*, and have even elaborated codes which classify and show the exact nature of the rewards and punishments which follow each sort of virtuous or evil deed.

This tendency to perceive in the Karman a sort of retributive justice, and to see it working as such in all the events of life, naturally gave rise to criticism. It is absurd, many Buddhists think, to establish a direct relation between the neuralgia or the intestinal troubles from which a man suffers and an evil deed which he once committed.

Milinda, in the work already quoted, interrogates Nâgasêna on the subject of various accidents and illnesses from which the Buddha suffered. Given the belief professed by Nâgasêna, this was to attack the most difficult side of the problem. What Nâgasêna really believed was not only that the Buddha was unable to do any further evil, since he had attained enlightenment, but also that all the consequences of such wrong acts as he had committed in the past were exhausted. How then was it possible for him to be ill, or how could he be hurt by a fragment of rock which his envious cousin had dropped upon him with murderous intent?

Evidently Nâgasêna could regard these facts as the action of Karman—of retributive justice—and as he could apparently envisage Karman only in this form, he denied that Karman was a general law.

'It is not true', replied Nâgasêna, 'that all suffering comes from the Karman. The bile, the fluids of the body, their combinations, the variations of temperature, the action of external agents, etc. . . . can produce suffering. Thus those who affirm that the Karman is the sole cause of suffering uphold an error.'

The king, who in the course of these dialogues often shows himself more subtle than his interlocutor, is by no means satisfied with this answer. Nâgasêna has referred the question back, but he has not answered it. All these details: bile, temperature, external agents, have a cause; their presence in the individual's organism, or in his environment: is it not attributable to the Karman?

Nâgasêna can only move yet another step backwards: 'The bile may be troubled by cold, by heat, by wrong food.' In such cases, the suffering would be the result of the cold, of the heat, or of unwholesome food. 'The number of events which are produced by Karman is small in comparison with those which other causes engender.'

Passing on to the accident of which the Buddha was a victim, Nâgasêna recalls the fact that Devadatta wished to kill his glorious cousin, of whose renown he was jealous. The rock which he rolled down the slopes of the mountain should, according to his calculations, have crushed the Buddha, who was seated lower down, but in rolling downwards the rock struck two others, and

was deflected from its course. The shock broke off a
fragment of stone which flew towards the Buddha and
struck him on the foot. The pain felt by the Master as
a result of this wound must have been an effect either
of his own Karman, or of causes unconnected with him
and his actions. Nâgasêna knows of no causes outside
these two categories, and as, according to him, the cause
of the painful accident could not be attributed to the
Karman of the Buddha, he declares that it was 'external'.
This conclusion is feeble, and not in accordance with the
spirit in which the king asked the question.

We should perhaps see in this dialogue the desire to
react against the idea which made people see in the
sick, the unhappy, the victims of any sort of ill fortune,
guilty individuals who were expiating their past faults.

This conception has not disappeared in India. One still
meets orthodox Hindus who hold to it. With the utmost
seriousness they will declare that to build hospitals, to
give alms to the poor, or in any way to relieve suffering,
is to go against the Law of Karman which produced
this suffering. Some will even go so far as to affirm that
such well-doing is harmful to those relieved by it,
because in mitigating their sorrows or freeing them
from suffering we retard the effects of their expiation.

To these unenlightened bigots one may object—and
Buddhists do not fail to do so—that if one admits that
the sick, the poor, and the unfortunate are suffering
the automatic penalty of old faults, one must also admit
that if the automatic result of this same Karman (their

past deeds) has brought them into contact with doctors
or generous persons who are willing and able to help
them, it has done so in order that they may profit by
such aid. If, according to this theory, their ills ought
to continue without alleviation, the force of their Karman
ought presumably to have led them far from any possible
source of help.

This logic will hardly convince those who are obstin-
ately attached to their cruel beliefs. It is a singular fact
that one meets individuals who apply this barbarous
faith to their own persons. Without being able to guess
what crimes they may have committed in their past lives,
without knowing for certain that they have ever committed any, these victims of a stupid dogma insist on
believing themselves guilty when stricken by physical
or moral suffering, and without reacting they submit
to their torments, seeing in them the expiation of faults
of which they are ignorant.

The manner in which Buddhism envisages the person
does not fit in with the ideas of strictly individual
retributive basis as they are generally understood in the
West. But in all countries men are readily illogical.
The most vehement defenders of the idea of personal
responsibility must, however, admit the law of heredity,
which 'visit the sins of the fathers upon the children
unto the third and fourth generation'.[1] On the other
hand, although they believe that the person is an aggregation of unstable elements, and that no soul or durable

[1] Exodus xx, 6.

'ego' can transmigrate from one life to the next, or be reincarnated in a new body, a large number of Buddhists continue to be haunted by the longing for individual retributive justice.

Let us return to Milinda. His dialogues with Nâgasêna epitomize the most orthodox Hinâyânist and semi-popular doctrine on the subject of Karman.

Milinda asked Nâgasêna:

'What is it which is reborn, Nâgasêna?'

'The Name and Form (the personality) is reborn.'[1]

'Is it the same Name and Form which is reborn?'

'No, but by this Name and Form actions are accomplished, good actions or evil actions, and, as a result of these, another Name and Form is born.'

'If it were thus, would not the new being be freed from his evil Karman?'

Nâgasêna replied: 'Yes, if he were not the product of a rebirth, but as he is such a product, he is not freed from his evil Karman.'

After which, Nâgasêna applies himself to proving that the new being, although different from the previous one, is its consequence, its prolongation.

A man taking a meal on the upper floor of his house allows his lamp to flare up too high, and set fire to the thatch of the roof. The whole house catches fire, and the fire passing from house to house, all the village is burnt.

---

[1] It agrees better with the meaning of the term to put the verb in the singular, for the couple forms an inseparable unity. We must remember that the *Name* represents those manifestations which constitute the mind; while the *Form* is the physical part of the person. See the preceding chapter.

The man is arrested, and they say to him: 'You have burnt the village'. But he replies: 'I have not burnt the village. The flame of the lamp which illuminated my repast was one thing, the fire which burnt the village was another'.

Nâgasêna, agreeing with Milinda, concluded that the man was to blame and should be punished, because the fire that destroyed the village came from the flame of his lamp.

In the ensuing discussion he propounds several comparisons of the same kind. I will note two of them:

'Imagine, O king, that a man pays a marriage-price to the parents of a little girl, intending to take her, later, as his wife; and then he goes elsewhere. In his absence the little girl grows up. Then another man pays a marriage-price to the parents, and marries the maiden. However, the first man returns and says: "Why have you married my wife?" But the new husband replies: "It is not your wife that I have taken . . ." '

The first man had chosen a little girl, the second had wedded a maiden of nubile age. In every way, physically and mentally, this latter differed from the little girl for whom the traveller had paid the price. Yet she was still herself.

'Imagine that someone buys a jug of milk from a cowherd and goes away, leaving the jug in his care, saying: "I will return tomorrow." And the following day the milk is curdled. When the buyer returns he is offered the curdled milk. He refuses it, saying: "It was not curdled milk that I bought from you; give me my jug of milk." But the cowherd replies: "With no intervention on my part, your milk has become curdled".'

Let us note, in passing, that in these two last comparisons Nâgasêna seems to incline toward the doctrines that consider the changes which have happened, whether to the milk or to the young girl, as representing the natural and continual evolution of a thing which still preserves a sort of basic identity. The curdled milk, the butter, the cheese, are only different aspects of the milk, as the little girl and the maiden are the successive aspects of the same woman.

This view was necessarily disputed by those Buddhists who held that the elements are not transformed, but disappear. I have heard it stated that these two opinions are not irreconcilable. It is, I was told, the serial succession (santâna) which causes the illusion of an individual thing. The nature of the elements which appear and disappear instantaneously determine the nature of those which will follow.

Whatever may be their value, all these theories, and the comparisons made to illustrate them, do not in fact reach to the bottom of the question. They may show the succession of causes and effects, but they do not in any way explain what these good people long to know: namely, that the mechanism of an equitable retribution gives our deeds a moral sanction by the harvest which we shall reap from them in future existences. Neither do they in any way prove that the happy or painful circumstances of our present life represent the result of our *personal* activity in the past.

This last idea is not found in Buddhism. When we meet it there we must attribute it to the lack of understanding, on the part of those who uphold it, of the Buddhist teaching. There can be no room for absolutely individual retribution in a philosophy which denies the permanence and reality of the individual.

Retribution can exist only in a collective form in the general Karman, just as the action which set it in motion was itself accomplished with the co-operation of the general Karman. Nâgasêna, in any case, could not fail to be aware of the intertwining of the currents of Karman.

Among the questions put by Milinda is one which concerns one of the numerous legends touching the previous existences of the Buddha (the Jatakas).

At this time, it is said, the future Buddha was a young Brahmin named Gotipâla. As Gotipâla, he insulted the Buddha Kasyapa, one of his predecessors. Invited to go and listen to his preaching, he replied to those who asked him: 'How can it benefit us to visit this good-for-nothing monk?'

Whence came the evil disposition that suggested these words to him? Here is what Nâgasêna said about it:

'The conduct of Gotipâla was due to his birth and to his family surroundings. He belonged to a family of unbelievers. His mother, his father, his sisters, his brothers,

his male and female relatives and his servants, were wor-
shippers of Brahma, followers of Brahma. Convinced
that the Brahmins were the noblest and most honourable
of men, he scorned those who had adopted the religious
life without belonging to their caste. It was under the
influence of what he had heard said around him that he
replied, when the potter Ghatikara invited him to visit
the Master: How can it benefit us to visit this good-for
nothing monk?'

The effects of education, according to Nâgasêna, here
prevailed over the good tendencies which the Buddha
possessed as the fruit of good actions which he had
accomplished in previous lives.

Even more complicated combinations appear in what
follows:

'Just as the best potion is bitter when it is mixed
with poison; just as the coldest water becomes hot on
contact with the fire; just as the hottest fire loses its
heat at contact with water, and is changed into cold,
black cinders, thus was it with Gotipâla. In spite of the
faith and knowledge which had been his (in previous
lives), when he was reborn into a family of unbelievers
he became as if blind.'

Nevertheless, underneath this sort of blindness the good
characteristics acquired in the course of past lives remain,
and are only waiting for a chance to show themselves.
It is thus that Gotipâla, having in the end gone to visit
Kasyapa, and having listened to his preaching, immediately understood the truth of his teaching, became his

disciple, and acquired higher powers of clairvoyance and concentration of thought.

If we accept the theories put forward in the *Bardo thöd dol*, a celebrated Tibetan work, the fact that Gotipâla was born in a family which was hostile to Buddhist doctrine showed that the tendencies towards unbelief had, by the power of affinities, led him thither. Thus, the cause of his conduct was not solely the unbelief of his family. A previous unbelief had combined with it to bring about this result.

Let us pass on from the Karman considered as a law of direct moral retribution, and consider some of its other aspects.

While Buddhism states that all things—objects, events, phenomena, facts of any kind—spring from a cause, it also affirms the complex character of the causes to which the result is due, and, further, it declares that these causes are interdependent.

If such and such things exist, then this or that other thing will arise. This is the formula of the 'Chain of Interdependent Origins' (pratîtyasamûtpâda), which we find again as the basis of the doctrine of Karman. But actually, the "Interdependent Origins' are only one aspect of Karman.

In a general way, Buddhism distinguishes three kinds of Karman, or of the relationship of the action to its result.

In the first place, there is the general Karman, which

perpetuates the round of existence (samsâra). Illusion, ignorance, desire in its two forms: attraction and repulsion, the thirst for existence which Professor Stcherbatsky has aptly called the *élan vital*: such are the causes to which this round is due. Here once more we come back to the doctrine of the 'Interdependent Origins'. The fundamental origin of illusion, of desire, of vital impulse, is declared to be unknowable.

'Unknowable is the beginning of beings wrapped in ignorance who, on account of their craving for existence, are led to ever-renewed births, and thus follow the round of rebirth' (Samyutta Nikâya).

The *Samyutta Nikâya*, a Hinayânist text, treats only of living beings, but according to a wider conception the thirst for existence, the *élan vital*, is the cause of existence of a stone no less than of a man or a god.

Plunged into the vortex of causes and effects, all beings tend to perpetuate it by their actions, and by their very existence, which is nothing but a series of activities. Let us recall what has been already stated: existence = activity. And activity, necessarily, must produce effects.

Then one may consider the Karman of so-called inanimate objects, which, as Karman special to the object, proceeds mechanically: appearance, growth, disintegration, disappearance. However, this special Karman, due to the particular nature of the object, is by no means independent of other Karmans. The period of existence normally allotted to a stone by its natural structure and the surroundings in which it is placed may be increased or diminished if the foot of a passer-by sends it rolling into the river, if it is removed to a place where the climatic conditions are different, if it is used in building a wall, or if it is placed in continual contact with the fire on a hearth.

The third kind of Karman, moral and intellectual Karman, applies to animate beings, and in their case it is additional to general Karman, and to the Karman of matter held to be inanimate.

We have seen that popular Buddhism concentrates its attention on this third kind of Karman, without seeming to perceive very clearly that the two other kinds of Karman exercise a constant influence over the moral and intellectual actions of the individual, just as these actions react on the general Karman, and on that of matter, and modify them.

The voluntary actions performed by an individual produce effects which may cause changes in the environment in which he lives, while the will, which is born in him, to perform these particular actions, is partly an effect of his surroundings (general Karman, including those actions committed in the past, and their results), and partly an effect of the physical constitution of his being (Karman of matter).

It is specially to be noted, in these theories, that voluntary action—and, according to some, any action of any kind, even involuntary—produces an alteration in the composition of the elements which make up the individual who has performed it.

At this point we may recall the seemingly incoherent reply which Yajñavalkya made to Artabhâga: Where is the man when he is dead; where does he go?

Yajñavalkya having led his questioner aside, so that no one should hear his answer, discussed Karman with him, and stated: 'By pure deeds man becomes pure; by evil deeds he becomes evil.'

Where is the man? Man is nothing but a bundle of activities, and these activities give rise to other groups of activities, which are beings. Pure deeds produce more pure deeds; evil deeds produce more evil deeds. They store up, in the general Karman, germs of happiness or of suffering respectively; they assemble, in this general Karman, the cause of the round of rebirth, complexes of energy tending to good actions and complexes of energy tending to evil actions, and these complexes are called, by us, beings, and appear to us as individuals.

Very probably Yajñavalkya did not intend to give his words a meaning which would agree with the Buddhist theory of the negation of the 'ego'; nevertheless, he declared that the action did transform the agent. Without attaching too great importance to this declaration of an almost mythical personality, a declaration which reflects the views of philosophers belonging to a rather vaguely defined period, it is still allowable to think that in very remote times there existed in India an esoteric doctrine of Karman widely different from that which is current in popular Buddhism and Hinduism. The idea of recompense and punishment without the intervention of any divine Judge does not exist in the esoteric doctrine, and is replaced by that of the transformation of the mental, and even the physical, substance.

I have already shown, in previous books,[1] that these theories are current in Tibet, and that the object of the mystical training there is precisely to bring about this transformation.

Regarded thus, the law of Karman assumes an exalted moral aspect. He who does good deeds is not paid for them by a reward which satisfies his more or less sensual desires: riches, celebrity, power, health, physical beauty, etc. The fruit of his pure, generous, and unselfish actions is his own improvement. Because he has acted with beneficence, he becomes better than he was before: his generous tendencies are strengthened, they show themselves more powerfully, and become habitual. In the same way, he who pursues knowledge will find that his taste for research increases, and his intelligence will develop. The man who is kindly and generous, the honest man, the man whose conduct is pure, will benefit from the state of mind which his conduct produces; he will be happy in becoming more and more inclined to good, and morally, better able to perform such actions with greater frequency and efficacy.

[1] *With Mystics and Magicians in Tibet* (John Lane, London), *Magic and Mystery in Tibet* (Claude Kendall, New York), *Initiations and Initiates in Tibet* (Rider, London).

On the other hand, cruel, stupid, and malevolent actions, and those which are inspired by sensuality, indolence, etc., will produce, in him who commits them, a gradual weakening of intelligence, benevolence, energy, etc. The consequence will be the tendency to accomplish such evil actions more and more frequently. If the man who has let himself slide down this slope does not react against his fall, he may become a demon; that is, according to the Tibetan conception, not an inhabitant of a special locality named Hell, but a particularly evil and malevolent being who can exist as a man in our world, or in any other form and in any other world, except the world of the gods where no evil may enter.

The greater the concentration of thought and the strength of will with which the action is first desired, and then decided upon, and finally accomplished, the deeper and wider are the changes which result in the composition of the agent. On the other hand, the greater the concentration of thought and the will, the more important and lasting are the effects of the action in the series of consequences which it engenders.

This is one of the reasons of the very important place which the concentration of thought and the will occupies in the Buddhistic methods of spiritual training.

Some regard the result that follows on a voluntary action as 'indifferent' for the author of the action, because the result is produced automatically, and as such does not appear to produce fresh karmic effects for him who performed the original voluntary action.

This opinion is rejected by others. According to them, as we have already seen, the involuntary action is productive of Karman, and so is the result, in whatever form it may appear, that follows the voluntary action; it takes its place in the 'series' of the latter.

Suppose that as the result of a deliberate murder a man is sent to gaol. The fact of being imprisoned—that is to say, the automatic result of the murder which he has committed—will exercise an influence on the prisoner and will induce physical or mental actions of one sort or another, which will continue the series of the effects of the murder.

In any case, the fact, whether of a mental or material order, automatically brought into being by the voluntary action, will take its place in the general Karman, and will thus exercise an indirect action on him who set it in motion.

The will which leads to the accomplishment of an action, moreover, is not, in Buddhism, considered as initial. It ranks as an effect, which becomes, in its turn, a cause, in a series of activities. This act of will has its antecedent causes, belonging to the general Karman, or connected with the actions which have been performed by him in whom it arose. Almost always it proceeds from these two factors, to which must be added the tendencies due to the physical and psychic composition of the individual.

As for the composition of his being, the individual owes it—as we have just said—to the action performed by him, but it has also been influenced by his association with other individuals. This applies especially to his father and mother. Generally, Buddhists believe that one is born (or rather *reborn*) to parents whose character has some resemblance to one's own character, either in the immediately anterior life, or in one or several anterior lives in the more distant past. According to this theory, it is the similarity of tendencies that produces the attraction, and the facts of heredity are thus explained in an inverse sense.

The multiplicity of the causes of the will reminds us of the parable quoted in the preceding chapter, in which a Tibetan lama described a person as being an assembly whose members have come from all parts of space.

To sum up, the individual, who can in no case be isolated and independent, is the result of the general Karman, of the cosmic Karman formed by the totality of the actions (Karman) which have been performed during a past to which there is no limit perceivable, and of those which are being performed at this very moment. The restricted Karman, envisaged as being constituted by the voluntary actions performed by the individual in his present life or in previous lives, is intimately bound up with the general Karman, and has no existence of its own outside this.

A picturesque comparison made by a lama described the interdependence of individual Karmans by comparing them to a multitude of flaming fires. Sparks rising from each fly through the air and fall into other fires, helping there to keep the fire going. Some of these fires throw out numerous and active sparks; others produce only small numbers of pale sparks. Some sparks travel a long way, and revive dying fires, or cause a terrible blaze by adding themselves to fires already burning furiously, while others fall into fires close to that from which they come. Between these extreme types all kinds of combinations can be imagined, but they will never approximate to the complexity of those which exist in reality.

In the same way, our words, our thoughts, the teachings which we propagate, the examples which we set, are so many sparks that spring from us and fall on others. Sometimes they penetrate into our neighbour's mind, sometimes into the mind of a man whose very existence is unknown to us, and who will receive them, at the other end of the world, through an account which he will hear, or a book which he will read, or again, as the Tibetans say: through the power of the 'waves that our actions and our thoughts create in the ether'.

And we, also, willingly or unwillingly, consciously or unconsciously, receive continually in ourselves the 'sparks' which have sprung from other living 'fires'.

There is not one single mental or material action which an individual can claim to be *entirely* his own work, just as there does not exist an individual who is not, mentally and physically, made up of the substance of others.

And what is the combustible which feeds the fires,

and whose sparks maintain the combustion? We come back once more to the fundamental doctrine of the 'Interdependent Origins'. The combustible is the ignorance-illusion without known beginning, that engenders desire within the fire, and the spark is the action (Karman) that keeps the fires burning.

Anticipating a question, although this perhaps is not the moment to consider it, one may ask: Why is the beginning of this ignorance, and in fact, the beginning of the round of existence, said to be unknown and unknowable? Buddhism replies: The ideas which we might conceive in respect of such a beginning would be the fruit of reasoning influenced by ignorance. All our ideas, even those which we call abstract, have their bases in perceptions and sensations due to the activity of the senses (the mind counting, among Buddhists, as a sixth sense). The power of the senses, as a means to understanding, is limited; it does not go beyond the world of relativity, and therefore the senses can only furnish information which is only relatively true. The facts which they perceive are true only for the man sunk in the 'round of existences' constituted by ignorance, desire, and action. All the speculations with which men have busied themselves on the subject of a first cause of the world of which they form a part have never been anything but the products of their own minds, nourished by that which exists in this world. They have been elaborated as in a closed container, within the circle of our private world, whose impassable frontiers are constituted by the limitations of our mental and physical means of perception.

In the *Lankâvatara Sutra*, a Mahâyânist work, an imaginary dialogue is recorded between the Buddha and a Bodhisatva named Mahâmati. In the course of this dialogue, Mahâmati asks the Buddha:

'I beg you, Venerable One, to explain to me that which causes all things?' (how things are caused, that is to say, came to be).

The Buddha replies:

'Mahâmati, there exist two causal factors by means of which all things come to be: the internal causes and the external causes.

'For example, the external causes may be a ball of clay, a stick, a wheel, a cord, some water, a workman and his work. The combination of all these things produces a pot.

'Just as for a pot made of clay, or a piece of cloth made of yarn, or a mat made of grass, or the shoot springing from a seed, or the butter produced from the milk churned by a man who works the churn—so is it for all things, which, being governed by external causes, spring up one after the other in a continual sequence. As for the internal factors which cause their appearance, these are: ignorance, desire, and action, which produce the idea of causation.'

This last statement agrees with Mahâyânist thought, which considers all doctrines from the point of view of relativity. The theory of causality is excellent, say the Mahâyanists; nothing is better fitted to make men distinguish the causes which produce suffering, and to lead them to fight these causes. Nor is anything more true, for man, than the teaching which explains to him the rigorous succession of causes and effects, and at the same time shows him their interdependence and their innumerable implications; yet this knowledge, although supremely profitable for man, must be regarded by him as relative. No theory can incorporate the absolute truth. Absolute truth is beyond our faculties of perception, and beyond our means of expression.

As I have shown in the chapter on the 'Twelve Interdependent Origins', the Tibetans have two words with the meaning of cause, and they generally couple them together; the first is *rgyu*, which means a principal cause; the second is *rkyen*, meaning a secondary cause. Lamaist teaching affirms the multiplicity of causes concerned in the production of each effect.

The following example is often given in Tibet: From the stone of an apricot a pine-tree will never result. The stone is the *rgyu*, the principal cause. Nevertheless, the development of the effects, whose usual end is the appearance of an apricot-tree, depends on the external Karman; that is to say, on secondary causes, *rkyen*. Among these latter are: the nature of the soil in which the stone is planted, the rainfall of that year (general Karman), which will water the kernel of the young shoot, the sunny or shady aspect of the spot where the sapling is growing, and the care which the gardener may take of the young tree, etc. A seed coming from a strong tree, and having in itself all the elements needed to produce another tree equally robust, may produce one which will remain feeble, or even one which will perish as a shoot, if the secondary causes are hostile to the development of the elements which constitute the seed, and the shoot which arises from it. Similarly, a mediocre seed may produce a tree which will grow strong if it is surrounded by favourable conditions. On the other hand, the general external Karman may be an obstacle in the way of the normal succession of the effects of the principal cause. The healthy seed, well fitted to grow into a tree, may perish in soil that is too hot and too dry; the young shoot may be crushed by the foot of a passer-by, or nibbled by a goat; and thus the tree, which a principal cause had destined to be born and to grow, will never exist.

This comparison can be applied to living beings; it is applicable to everything, in the realm of the mind as in that of matter; in all cases a principal cause encounters the action of other factors, some of which are in harmony with it and aid it, while others obstruct it.

Can the belief in free-will harmonize with the doctrine of Karman? If one means by free-will the power to act absolutely as one wishes, and to *will* absolutely as one *wills*, the only reply is a categorical negative. But only those who avoid reflection still believe in this kind of free-will.

A Chinese once said to me, laughing: 'I am certainly
not free to touch the ceiling. My arm is not long enough
to allow it. All the same, I can make use of various
methods; I can climb on to a chair, or artificially elongate
my arm by holding a stick in my hand.'

There are means of modifying a determined series of
effects by combining this series with another series of
effects. Thus all fatalism is excluded from this doctrine
of Karman. Of course, every effect springs from causes,
and every action, whether physical or mental, is a cause
which must infallibly be followed by effects; yet between
the moment when the cause arises and the moment when
that which we consider as its direct effect is seen, numerous
relations with other currents of cause and effect take
place, without our being conscious of them, and the
exact result of these combinations is difficult to foresee.
It is even truer to say that it cannot be foreseen, for
although there is determinism here, the combinations
which this latter may bring about are infinite in number,
and therefore quite unpredictable; except perhaps in
broad outlines.

Man is dependent on the general Karman of humanity,
and he is also dependent on the cosmic Karman. If a
man finds himself caught in the midst of a war, or an
epidemic of plague, or if a cataclysm, such as an earth-
quake, occurs in the place where he is living, the sequence
of his own deeds, and perhaps his character, will be
altered by these circumstances. Some Buddhists will say
that past deeds have led the man to be born in the place

where these calamities were going to happen, or perhaps to move to it if the place of his birth was destined to be immune to such troubles. Even if one admits this, it is nevertheless true that the Karman appertaining to the individual (if a strictly individual Karman can exist) is intimately bound up with the general Karman.

Let us see what contemporary Buddhists have to say on this point. Here is an extract from a work[1] by Professor Narasu of Madras:

'All creatures are such as they are through past *samskaras* (mental formations, activities), and when they die their life shapes new beings. In the slow process of evolution activities shape new personalities. What is called the person is but the living embodiment of past activities, physical and psychical. Past activities impress upon creatures the nature of their present existence. This is the law of Karman as understood in Buddhism. No other interpretation of the doctrine of Karman can be consistent with the teaching of the Blessed One as to the momentaneity and the unsubstantiality of all existing things (unsubstantiality, because they exist only in dependence on other things).

'That in the personal development of each individual every thought, or feeling, or volition counts for something is not difficult to perceive, but that there is a retribution after death, when there is no transmigrating *atman* (ego), can have no meaning and validity apart from the individual's relation to mankind as a whole.

[1] *The Essence of Buddhism.*

'Physiologically considered, an individual is reincarnated in his progeny, and his physical Karman is transmitted to them. Ethically considered, the psychic life of an individual cannot be separated from the psychic life of the community of which he is a member. Duty and responsibility have no meaning apart from society. How, then, can a man have Karman apart from other human beings? The enjoyments and sufferings of an individual are not always the result of his special Karman' (of deeds which he himself has done).

'The *Milindapañha* (Questions of King Milinda) tells us that it is an erroneous extension of the truth when the ignorant declare that "every pain is the fruit of (individual) Karman." Yet no Buddhist will deny that everything is under the sway of causality. Unless we regard all mankind as linked together as parts of one universal whole, we cannot perceive the full significance of the doctrine of Karman. Not only are the murderer and the thief responsible to society, but society is equally responsible for breeding such characters. . . .

'. . . The Buddhist doctrine of Karma differs totally from the Brahmanic theory of transmigration. Brahmanism teaches the transmigration of a real soul, an *atman*, but the Dharma indicates a mere succession of Karmas. (A series of acts and results following one another to infinity.) According to the Brahmanic conceptions the soul migrates from man to one or other of the so-called "six kingdoms", from man to animal, from animal to hell, from hell to heaven, and so forth, just as a man migrates from one house to another according to his necessities. It may indeed be true that in the Buddhist sutras also there are references to a transmigration to one or other of the "ten worlds", but this does not mean that any being passes from one world to another. For the real Buddhist, paradises and hells are in no way real places, but imaginary creations of ignorant minds.[1]

'In the Buddhist sense transmigration is only a manifestation of cause and effect. Only by virtue of causes and conditions are produced mental phenomena accompanied by bodily forms, and thus results life after life, the nature and character of the successive lives being determined by the goodness or badness of the mental phenomena. It is to explain and illustrate the transmigration of Karman to the ordinary man that the Blessed One employed the expression "ten worlds", while really he meant by the "ten worlds" nothing more than the ten mental states typified by the beings and places referred to.'

The opinion of Professor Narasu as regards the hells is perfectly orthodox, especially among the Mahâyânists, to which philosophical school he belongs. Looking through the Buddhist Scriptures we find very definite statements on this subject:

'Hell has not been created by anyone. The fire of a

[1] Candrakîrti, a disciple of Nâgârjuna, holds the same opinion. To support it, in his commentary on Nâgârjuna's *Treatise on Relativity*, he quotes a passage of the *Vajramandaradharani*: 'The hells are produced by imagination. Fools and simple people are cheated by error and illusion. . . . And the delightful heavenly palaces are also constructed by imagination.'

mind which gives itself up to anger produces the fire of hell and consumes him who possesses it. When a man does evil, he lights the fire of hell and burns himself in his own fire.' (Mulamuli.)

An anecdote of which Bodhidharma[1] is the hero tells how he discussed the question of the existence of hell with a Chinese prince who denied it, while Bodhidharma persisted in affirming it. The argument continuing, the prince became heated, and lost his self-control on being disrespectfully contradicted by his opponent; infuriated and unable to contain himself, he insulted Bodhidharma, who, seeing him so enraged, calmly told him once more: 'Hell exists and you are in it'.

Again, in a Mahâyânist work called *Vajramanda-dhârani*, in which the Buddha is supposed to hold converse with Manjuçri, we read:

'The hells, O Manjuçri, are products of the imagination. Stupid and ignorant people are deceived by error and illusion.'[2]

A Japanese, Kuroda, writes of Karman: 'There is neither creator nor created, and men are in no way real beings (have no permanent ego). That is to say: they are not autogenous, they are produced by causes, and they are a group of impermanent elements.[3] Actions are

[1] Bodhidharma was a Brahmin from Southern India. He went to China about A.D. 500 to preach Buddhism. He was the founder of the 'Meditation' sect; T'san, in Chinese; Zen in Japanese. The anecdote here related is reported also, with somewhat different details, in respect of several spiritual Masters.

[2] See footnote page 201.

[3] See the meaning, in Buddhism, of the term 'real', page 137.

the causes which, under favourable conditions, give birth to them. Men are nothing more than the temporary combination of five *skandhas* or constituent elements (1, Form. 2, Perception. 3, Sensation. 4, Confections, or mental formations. 5, Consciousness). The beginning of the combination is their birth, its dissolution is their death. While the state of combination continues good and bad actions are performed, and precisely by this the seed of future joys and future sorrows is sown, and in this way the alternations of birth and death follow endlessly.

'Men are not real beings who of themselves wander from birth to death, nor does there exist any authority which makes them move in this way; it is their own actions that produce this result. It is from the combined action of animated beings that mountains, rivers, lands, etc., arise. All these things which are caused by combined action are, consequently, called *adhipatiphala* (combined or united fruits). . . .

'. . . Each man receives a mind and a body corresponding to the causes which are in operation, the interior causes of actions being favoured by external conditions. . . .

'. . . The period between the beginning of life and death, during which the body persists, makes up the life of a man, just as that period stretching from formation to destruction, during which mountains, rivers, continents, etc., preserve the same form, constitutes the duration of these latter. The alternation, among animated beings, of birth and death, like the formation and destruction of mountains, rivers, continents, etc., is endless in its action. Just as the circle has no end, neither has this chain beginning or end.

'Although neither real beings nor real things exist, yet effects appear and disappear where the necessary actions and conditions meet, as the echo follows the sound, and all things coarse or fine, large or small, come and go at every instant, without any permanent form. Men and things are just words, indicating the length of time during which a given form persists. Our present life is the reflection of past actions. Men consider this reflection as their real "ego". They imagine as objects belonging to them their eyes, their noses, their ears, their tongues, their bodies, like their gardens, their woods, their farms, their houses, their workmen and their servants, but in reality all these things are only results produced *ad infinitum* by innumerable actions.' (Kuroda: Outlines of Mahâyâna.)

In order to avoid any misunderstanding of what the author says of the *duration* of things, and especially of human beings, it must be remembered that in Buddhism this apparent duration is made up of a succession of momentary phenomena which appear only to disappear, each bringing about, by its disappearance, the following phenomenon.

'What is the duration of human life?' asked the Buddha of one of his disciples. 'The time of a breath,' replied the latter, and the Buddha approved the reply: 'It is well, my son; thou art already advanced on the path.' (Sutra in Forty-Two Sections.)

Others say: Life lasts as long as a thought. When the thought disappears, the life of the being is over, and that which takes its place is a different being, although resulting from that which preceded it.

And: 'That which we call mind, or thought, or knowledge, is produced and disappears in a perpetual change.'

These theories have already been mentioned, in the section concerning the 'ego'.

Must a man inevitably suffer the effects of the actions which he has performed? We have already seen that many subsidiary causes may modify these effects, or even prevent their production, but here we are concerned with something else, with an act of the will. He who has committed a particular action, or who has decided to commit one, can he, if he so desires, find means to prevent or to soften the consequences? Not all Buddhists are in agreement on this point.

'There does not exist in this world, neither in the air, nor in the midst of the ocean, nor in the depths of the mountains, a place where one can free oneself from the evil which one has done.' (Dhammapada.)

This strictness is not acceptable to all. Few men have sufficient strength and dignity always to accept full responsibility for their actions, and to face their consequences without weakening. Once the deed has been done, under the impulse of desire—envy, love, or hate—

its author, if he believes in retributive justice, often shrinks from the penalties of the latter. What then occupies his mind is not so much regret for his conduct, because of the ill done *to others*, as the aftermath of unpleasant results which it may cause *to himself*.

It is the same in all countries, and the faithful of all religions zealously resort to the means which these religions have devised by which they may be spared the threatened punishments.

Popular Buddhism is no exception. Incapable of rising to the level of the philosophy of the Sage whom they call their Master, the Buddhists, like the followers of other religions, have devised ritual acts which are regarded as capable of warding off the threatened consequences of their faults.

At a higher plane of understanding the Buddhists attempt to counterbalance the results of their wrong actions by setting against them actions of the opposite sort. For example, the deplorable effects of miserliness, or a lack of generosity, will be outweighed by the charity which makes the person concerned distribute a large amount of alms. Actions inspired by ill-will, pride, anger, etc., will be counterbalanced by actions inspired by goodwill, humility, tolerance, patience, etc.

In this manner those whom the Buddhist Scriptures call 'children' or 'fools' (bâla) reassure themselves. Such people do not know that the Buddhist doctrine regards the material act as of much less value than the mental act. Far from attaining the desired goal through their good works, they only accentuate the bad aspects of their character, if these works are undertaken by them in the egotistical hope of escaping from the penalties which their cowardice makes them dread. These good works, if they are to soften the effects of past wrong actions, must spring from a change of mind, leading the individual to renounce his old habits and to adopt others of an opposite kind, because he judges that these latter are superior.

In order that the 'transmutation' of which I have already spoken may take place it is essential that the change of conduct should have its source in a mental change, and that the new direction given to one's acts should be continuously maintained. Above all, it is necessary that this should not be done as a bargain; good actions should be performed for the love of good actions, even if they do not in any way soften the painful effects of the evil actions which their author has previously committed.

This is a sentiment which comes very close to perfect contrition as it is defined by the Catholic Church, but as Buddhists deny the existence of a supreme and personal god there can be, for them, no question of having offended him. A Buddhist, if he repents, repents for having caused suffering to another; or perhaps he regrets that he lowered himself to commit actions which, as he considers them from a new point of view, appear to him vile or stupid.

But does a genuine Buddhist repent? One may reply

in the negative. A profound understanding of the doctrine of Karman and the perception of the momentariness of the elements to which all phenomena are due— including the manifestations of our activity—make him consider this kind of return to the past quite useless.

Once accomplished, the action gives rise, immediately, to a series of effects of which each in its turn becomes a cause, and produces a new series of effects. It is with actions as it is with the bullet which has left the rifle: the firer can neither catch it again nor can he influence its course. The knowledge of his own powerlessness in such questions leads the Buddhist not lightly to set in motion, in the world, a series of causes and effects which, his action once performed, escape for ever from his control.

Among the Buddhists only those who are still at the lower levels of understanding of the Doctrine, and who believe in an *individual* retribution for actions, try to keep a sort of account-book of their actions, and busy themselves in accumulating merits and in making up for their demerits. My experience, gained during a large number of years spent in different Buddhist countries, compels me to say that these good account-keepers, these merchants anxious to receive, either in this life or in another, the exact payment due to them for their works, form the majority of the faithful. Is it not, in any case, the same in all religions? However this may be, the more enlightened Buddhist, more deeply affected by the spirit of the Buddhist Doctrine, does not childishly attempt to undo that which is done; he does not dwell on the desire that that which has been might not have been; and, on the other hand, he does not seek any personal reward. Or, rather, he finds his reward in the satisfaction which he feels when he has rendered some living being happy.

'I seek no reward, not even to be reborn in the celestial worlds, but I seek the well-being of men, I seek to bring back those who have gone astray, to enlighten those who live in the darkness of error, to banish from the world all sorrow and all suffering.' (Fo-cho-hing-tsan king.)

We have seen in a previous chapter that the Buddhist is advised to examine the results of his actions as far as he is capable of following them, and to abstain from committing afresh those which he judges to be bad. If he considers them bad, this should be because he has perceived their harmful results, and not because these deeds violate a code of morality which has been formulated by a god or by an illustrious sage, or which derives its authority simply from the general consent of mankind. This has been explained in the section on morality.

There is thus, in Buddhism, no place for sentimental contrition or dramatic repentance. Both are regarded as not only useless but harmful, because they arise from the false idea that most men hold of their importance in the universe, and flatter their vanity by allowing them to think that heaven and earth are interested in their tiny misdeeds.

Among those Buddhists—especially in Tibet—who have incorporated with the Mahâyânist doctrines various elements of Tantric origin, one meets with curious methods which aim at obstructing those automatic Karmic penalties that might cause mental degradation and create affinities of an inferior order, likely to lead towards what are symbolically named the worlds of darkness and suffering.

These methods, at least in their simplest form, bear only upon those notions which directly concern no one but their authors. Sensuality, laziness, gluttony, intemperance, etc. . . . come under this category, and the actions which they inspire are called 'bodily acts'. It is said that he who in cold blood decides to commit a bodily action of the sort known as bad, should, with calm forethought, provide beforehand against the results—other than bodily— which this action will provoke. He will gain his ends by effecting a sort of doubling of his personality, by preventing the physical sensations which he is seeking from exercising any influence on his mind, and from arousing in this latter any adhesion, any participation which would constitute a 'mental act' superposing itself on the 'bodily act'. This mental act must not be allowed to come into being, in order to prevent the consequences, which would be a modification, a change for the worse, in the elements forming the mental part of the personality.

Adepts of these theories pretend that they are capable of feeling, in the highest degree, all physical joys and sufferings while keeping their mind perfectly free from their influence, and without quitting the position of interested onlooker, sometimes ironic or scornful, but always detached.

According to the idea which is current in the West, want of intention and of knowledge of the importance of an action reduce the culpability of the sinner. To sin from ignorance seems less serious than to sin knowingly, and should therefore need a lighter penalty.

Tibet, and, before Tibet, India, have seen the matter quite differently.

'Milinda asked Nâgasêna: Who has the greater demerit: he who sins knowingly, or he who sins inadvertently?'

'He who sins inadvertently.'

'In this case, Reverend, we should doubly punish one of our family or of our Court who has done wrong unintentionally.'

'How think you, O King, if a man intentionally grasped a mass of hot metal, and if another took hold of it unintentionally, which of these two would be the most burnt?'

'He who did not know what he was doing.'

'It is the same also with the man who is ignorant of what he is doing.' (Questions of Milinda.)

The term 'demerit', here, should be understood in its Buddhist meaning, that is to say, as injurious result produced by the law of Karman. That is why the example

---

¹ We find signs of an analogous doctrine in Brahmanist parables: 'Two birds always united, of equal name, dwell upon one and the same tree. The one of them enjoys the sweet fruit of the fig tree, the other looks round as a witness.' (Mundaka Upanishad III, I, I, and Swetaswatara Upanishad IV, 6.)

given by the king has no relation to the question. Certainly the king would be right to show indulgence toward one who disobeyed inadvertently the orders he had given him, or the law which he had established for all his subjects, but this was not the question.

He who is preparing to touch a piece of glowing metal can take precautions to reduce or neutralize the natural effect of its contact with his flesh. He can cover his hands with some thick material soaked in water, or make use of some other expedient. The unreflecting man, on the contrary, will put his hand directly on the hot iron and will suffer agonizing pain.

Thus certain wrong actions may, in principle, be rendered less harmful by the use of means to attenuate their unpleasant results, or to prevent them from occurring.

Evidently the man who takes the laws of morality as being the expression of the will of a god, and who sees in each breach of these laws a personal offence done to this god, must consider as frightful and devilish wickedness the art of cleverly sinning while protecting oneself from punishment. But the law of Karman does not proceed from any divine law-maker; it is an automatic process; consequently, to make use of it in order to oppose one cause to another, in order to make one effect offset another, does not constitute an offence to anyone.

It must be added that this particular 'science' can liberate its practitioner only from the direct and quite personal results of his deed. As to that part of the results which his actions have sent forth into the general Karman, he cannot avoid feeling their influence.

But how does the desire to 'trick' Karman arise in man? It cannot exist without a cause, and, in fact, this decision to interfere with the action of Karman is, itself, a product of Karman.

This conclusion brings us back to the problem of free will. Let us once more see what a Buddhist, Professor Narasu, has to say on this point.

'The will is a state of conscience resulting from the co-ordination, more or less complex, of a certain number of psychic and physiological states which, all united, express themselves by an act or by an abstention. The principal factor in this co-ordination is the character, an extremely complex product, formed by heredity, ante-natal and post-natal psychological conditions, education, and experience.

'One part only of this psychological activity is known to us under the form of deliberation. The acts and the movements which follow on deliberation result directly from the tendencies and feelings, images and ideas which have become co-ordinated in the form of a choice. Choice is, therefore, not the cause of anything, but is itself an effect.

'. . . If the will were free, it would be impossible to change our character by education. But experience teaches that a man's character is composed of various qualities, and is modifiable by a certain sequence of efforts. For this reason, because man's will obeys motives and is dependent on causes, he can be made to transform himself by changing his surroundings, his manner of life, and by guiding, with due reflection, the motives of his will.'[1]

Supported by theories similar to those of the author just quoted, a casuist of the Dzogschen Sect would say: 'This desire to check the current of effects springing from deeds already accomplished arises from causes, and one may believe that the nature of these latter is such that they already constitute an obstacle to the results it is desired to prevent.'

Thus, according to this opinion, the will to oppose the law of Karman, and the means employed to reach this end, are only tangible manifestations of forces which, already, tended automatically to appear in the development of the effects natural to actions performed, and to modify the form and the range of these effects.

The Tibetans, as is well known, have elaborated a particular kind of Buddhism consisting of Mahâyânist doctrines, as regarded from their standpoint as a yellow race, with the addition of a basis of theories and psychological and magical sciences inherited from unknown ancestors. This is what the Orientalists call 'Lamaism', a curiously extensive mosaic, hiding unexplored depths. Among the doctrines grafted on to those of Buddhism, I will here quote only that which bears directly on my present subject. It concerns the possibility of freeing oneself, completely or partially, *after death*, from the un-

[1] L. Narasu, *The Essence of Buddhism*.

pleasant consequences of past misdeeds, and of obtaining either deliverance from the circle of rebirth, or a happy rebirth, *in spite* of the Karman.

The spiritual leaders of Tibet teach their disciples the means to attain this end. On the other hand, there are in existence works which explain, more or less summarily, the existing theories on this subject. Among such is the *Bardo thöd dol.*

Of the origin of this treatise we know only what we learn from tradition, strongly coloured by the marvellous, and therefore suspect. We are told that the author of the *Bardo thöd dol* was Padmasambhava, the magician who dwelt in Tibet in the eighth century, and there preached a Mahâyânist Buddhism mingled with Tantric doctrines. Padmasambhava is believed to have composed a considerable number of works which he afterwards hid, judging that the Tibetans of his time were not yet able to understand them. In the course of centuries these *termas* (from *ter*, written *gter*, and meaning treasure) were found, here and there, by seers or other individuals supposed to possess supernormal faculties. In some cases the birth of these people had been foretold by Padmasambhava, and some of them are held to have been Padmasambhava himself reincarnated.

The number of works regarded as *termas* runs into hundreds. Over and above those whose authenticity, although very debatable, is officially recognized in Tibet, many others exist of which the origin is not always attributed to Padmasambhava. The authors of some are said to be famous lamas, others are supposed to have been composed by deities of the Lamaist pantheon, or by gods or heroes belonging to the Bonpo religion. Thus, in the north and east of Tibet individuals thought to be clair-voyant search for the *termas* hidden by the great national hero Gesar of Ling.[1] Some *termas* consist of only a few lines, others are relatively voluminous books. Among the rarest, those of which one speaks in mysterious whispers, are instructions engraved on stone which have been found or dug up in a 'miraculous' fashion.

Among the less celebrated *termas* are some which are profoundly interesting to the student of philosophy or of methods of psychic training. These are often written in a conventional and symbolic language understood only by initiates, and which may perhaps constitute the last relics of a special language, related to a pre-Buddhist esoteric doctrine. The majority of *termas*, however, con-tain only statements of doctrines familiar throughout Tibet; or in some cases they are composed of loosely connected phrases written in a debased Sanskrit, almost, if not quite, unintelligible, and copiously interspersed with ritual exclamations, like the monosyllabic *mantrams*.

The opinion is prevalent among the people and the lower clergy of Tibet that many *termas* still remain to be discovered.

The origin of the *termas* is still regarded with discreet

---

[1] About this hero, see *The Superhuman Life of Gesar of Ling*, which I have translated from the songs of Tibetan bards. (Rivers, London; and Claude Kendall, New York.)

scepticism by the élite of the lamas. Examples are quoted of lamas who, being greedy for celebrity, have hidden manuscripts of their own composition, in order to 'discover' them later, and so merit the title of *tértön* (discoverer of a *terma*), which among the masses is much more highly regarded than that of author. Hardly a single year passes in which one or more of these mysterious works are not discovered in caves or other solitary places.

It would be irrelevant in this present volume to tell how I made a discovery of this kind. I will do so elsewhere.

My old travelling companion and fellow student, the scholarly Tibetan, Dawasandup, in whose company I have ridden so far in the Himalayas, going from one monastery to another, has made an English translation of one of the versions of the *Bardo thöd dol*. This translation was edited by a learned American Orientalist, W. Y. Evans-Wentz, who has added to it an erudite introduction and numerous notes, forming an excellent commentary.

The *Bardo thöd dol*, and all works of this kind, are regarded by Tibetan scholars as the exoteric expression of esotoric theories concerning death, its accompanying phenomena, and those which follow it, between the moment when the man dies and that of his rebirth. *Bardo* means 'between two'—between death and rebirth.

In Tibet the art of dying skilfully—and, I will add, *profitably*—is considered of the highest importance;

Buddhists and Bonpos teach it in one form or another, but always under two aspects: the exoteric, divulged in books—*termas* or others—and the esoteric, which is communicated by word of mouth, permission being sometimes given to the disciples to take written notes of a few of the points taught, to assist their memory.

The Bonpos pretend that it is from them that Padmasambhava and the other Buddhist authors who have written on this subject have borrowed their theories. They also boast freely of possessing physiological and psychological knowledge dating back to remote antiquity, and far exceeding in extent and profundity that of the Buddhists. I leave the responsibility for these statements to those who made them to me, but it may well be that they are not entirely without foundation.

Buddhists, both Hinayânists and Mahâyânists, attach great importance to the last thought of a dying person. They believe that it is this thought which gives the tone, the general direction, to the new life which the dying man will begin with his rebirth. The effects of Karman will none the less be felt, but they will follow the effect of this last thought, and will be modified by its influence. Among the Tibetans the influence of this last thought is generally recognized, but more especially among the mass of the unlearned believers. However, these are exhorted to form thoughts of *detachment* from the world from which they are about to depart, rather than virtuous thoughts, apart from a sincere wish for the happiness of living beings. As for more enlightened individuals, and those who have received a few lessons from a spiritual master, they are specially recommended to overcome the loss of consciousness which usually occurs at the moment of death, and to perceive clearly the phenomenon of the passing of the consciousness out of this life.

Advice to this effect is whispered into the ears of all dying people who have, at their bedside, either a lama, or a layman knowing something of 'the art of dying,' but it is presumed that those who during life have not prepared themselves for this moment are unable to make the effort required to avoid the loss of consciousness at the moment of death.

Why is it necessary to die with full consciousness?— Simply to prevent the automatic operation of Karman, just as those endeavour to do, during their lifetime, who have acquired 'skill in means' (upaya) based on knowledge of the mechanism of Karman. Apart from the contemplative hermits and lamas familiar with the teachings of the spiritual masters, very few people die fully conscious. According to a belief which is widespread not only in Tibet, but also in Nepal and India, among Buddhists and the adepts of other doctrines, the man who dies in a swoon recovers from this latter not exactly in another world, but in another condition: in what the Tibetans call the 'intermediate state' (bardo).

What is that which after death recovers consciousness, and which is bound to experience the results of the actions performed by the dead man?—Among non-Buddhists the reply is simple; that which continues to exist beyond death is the *jiva*, the spirit, an immortal entity very like that which we call the 'soul'.

Their attachment to the idea of an entirely individual retribution for actions performed has led the majority of Buddhists to form conceptions which approximate to the belief in the transmigration of the spirit, although for them the 'spirit' is not a simple entity, but an aggregate of mental faculties, as has been explained in the preceding chapter. The spirit is not regarded as the possessor of these faculties, itself existing apart from them; it is not *endowed* with the power of perception, of wishing, etc.; but when perceptions, sensations, constructive mental operations and consciousness *exist*, the sum of this activity, made up of different components, takes the name of spirit.

According to the lamaists, however, that which enters into the intermediate state (*bardo*) is only one of the parts which makes up the spirit: it is the consciousness, which contains, in itself, the sum of impressions which have been stored in the 'conscious' and 'subconscious' mind of the individual during his past life.

The Tibetans, and some of their neighbours in India and Nepal, hold that the 'consciousness' of the ordinary man dying during a swoon, without understanding what has happened to him, finds itself very much at a loss in its new state. It does not know of the change which has taken place in its condition; it is troubled and alarmed, while it tries unsuccessfully to reoccupy the place in this world which belonged to it during the lifetime of the body to which it was attached. In this agitated state the power to direct itself, to resist the pressure of Karman which is acting on it, is lacking. Others will come to its help.

Already, during the death-agony, the lama or the competent layman who is with the dying man has strongly advised him to let his 'consciousness' escape through the crown of his head, for any other exit would lead to a bad rebirth. But here again, the dying man, if he has had no special training, is incapable of helping himself, and the rite of 'transference' intervenes. In Tibetan this rite is called *phowa* (pronounced *powa*, from *pho*, to move to another place, to transfer). The essential part of *phowa* consists in the ejaculation, in a very special and piercing tone, of the syllable *hik*,[1] followed by the syllable *phat*. These two syllables are held to be *mantrams*: that is to say, words whose vibrations—if the sound has been correctly emitted—have the power to produce certain effects on the mind and on matter.

In theory, the *hik*, several times repeated, causes the 'consciousness' gradually to rise to the crown of the head, and *phat* makes it burst out of the skull. It happens at times that Tibetan mystics practise this rite for themselves, in order to commit suicide, just as certain Hindu yogis suffocate themselves voluntarily by holding their breath while in trance. However, according to the worthy people of Tibet, the action of *phowa* is not limited to

[1] On this subject see my books: *Among the Mystics and Magicians of Tibet*, or *Magic and Mystery in Tibet*.

extracting the consciousness from the body of the dying man, or from the dead man from whose body its exit is delayed; it will also transfer the consciousness to a place of bliss, generally to the Western Paradise of the Great Beatitude (*Nub Dewachen*, in Sanskrit, *Sukhavati*), of which the Buddhist masses in China and Japan also dream.

In reality, the use of *phowa* to guide the 'consciousness' of the dead verges upon the magic science of 'transference' or 'resurrection'. This consists in separating the mental part of the personality—one's own or that of another—and transferring it, temporarily or permanently, into a human or animal body. This body may be one which has been abandoned, at the moment of death, by the spirit which had been joined to it, or one from which the magician has dislodged the spirit by force. In this latter case the magician may transfer the homeless spirit into a recently dead body, if he can find one available, or he may evict another spirit from its home, so as to provide shelter for the first, or, finally, he may leave the spirit disincarnated, a condition which is said to be very painful for the latter. Stories of 'transferences' are numerous in Tibet, but the methods by which they are practised are taught only to a very few disciples after a long probationary period, and under the seal of secrecy, guarded by awe-inspiring oaths. This so-styled science of transference is also known in China and India.

As for the ascent of the 'consciousness' to the summit of the skull, this is borrowed from the Tantric theories concerning the vital energy symbolized by *kundalini*, the fiery serpent, which sleeps near the organs of generation, and which the yogis awaken and cause to ascend to the brain through various points in the body (the *chakras* = wheels) and along the vertebral column. This ascent is regarded as a physical reality, or as being symbolic, according to the degree of Tantric initiation.

Among those Buddhists who admit the existence of the intermediate state there are some who do not accept the idea of a transference operated by the agency of another person. Most, however, believe that the 'consciousness' itself may possibly pass through the *bardo* toward a chosen rebirth. Theoretically, then, it may attain to one or other of the worlds of the gods, or enter into a human body, choosing, as its parents, those whose character and condition are such as to assure the moral and material well-being of the child whom they will beget. Further, some believe in the possibility of succeeding, after death, in a moment of sudden illumination of the discarnate 'consciousness', in enfranchising themselves from the round of repeated births and deaths; that is to say, in liberating themselves definitely from all effects of Karman.

These various possibilities are naturally based on the belief in the continuance of the consciousness after death. This 'consciousness', then, is regarded as an entity, a receptacle in which are stored all the moments of consciousness which have succeeded one another during the life of the deceased. At the same time, it is supposed to enjoy the power of perception, of reasoning about its perceptions, and of receiving impressions. Thus envisaged, the 'consciousness' offers points of resemblance to the 'double', although the Tibetans regard it as distinct from the latter. It resembles the soul, or the Hindu *jiva*, with this striking difference, however, that it is not immortal, its existence ending with the rebirth which is the beginning of the formation of a new consciousness, depending on the organs of perception, sensation, etc., which will supply it with aliment. One must nevertheless remember that according to this theory the conditions of rebirth, the physical form, and the mental qualities of the new individual are conditioned by the preceding consciousness.

Deprived, after death, of the perceptions which the senses transmitted to it, and which nourished it, the disincarnate 'consciousness' *ruminates*, if I may use this trivial but exact expression, on the ideas which have been accumulated in it during the lifetime of the physical and mental aggregation (called a person) of which it formed a part. The visions which it sees, which disconcert, or stupefy, or delight, or terrify it, are nothing but subjective images, projected by itself, and illustrating its own beliefs, its passions, and, in general, all the content of the mind of the deceased.

To discern, in this chaos of images, those which emanate from currents of energy productive of happy conditions, and those which are due to certain of its own affinities, and which bear it toward environments that will be agreeable to it, is an art which very few 'consciousnesses' possess. So on this occasion the dead man receives the help of one of the living, who explains to him the nature of the visions which are supposed to appear to him, and points out to him how he should bear himself toward them.

Yet choosing between the routes and the beings which appear in these visions is regarded as the effect of knowledge of an inferior order. The secret which brings about the supreme deliverance in the *bardo* is the knowledge of the fundamental unreality of the scenes which are held there, of the beings which are encountered there, of the joys which are enjoyed there, and of the sorrows which are suffered there. The 'consciousness' must know that this mirage, as we have seen, is an objectification of its thoughts, that it exists *in* these thoughts, and nowhere outside them.

This last theory is in complete conformity with the doctrine of the idealistic school of Buddhism. This doctrine, which does not accept the conception of the *bardo*, declares that deliverance from the round of 'existences' consists in understanding, in this life, that the *samsâra*, with its various worlds, its gods, its demons, its paradises, its hells, and all the beings which there suffer, enjoy, love, hate, fight, are born, and die, is merely a product of our imagination, a huge mystification due to ignorance, an hallucination produced by the longing for individual existence.

An opinion fairly widespread among learned lamas is

that the same possibilities of deliverance *post mortem* are open to all, whatever may have been their religion, or the philosophical doctrines which they professed during their lifetime.

A lama belonging to the monastery of Ditza, situated near the Chinese frontier, who had had the opportunity of meeting Christian missionaries, and learning something of their doctrine, told me one day that the judgment, heaven, and hell awaited them in the *bardo*. According to him, the Christians, like the Lamaists, would furnish their 'intermediate state' with visions in accordance with their beliefs; they would see there God the Father, Jesus, angels, and the saints and demons, which would, no doubt, have been especially present in their minds at the hour of death. They would suffer or rejoice according to the nature of their visions, which they would imagine to be realities, until the moment when a swoon, like that in which they died, would mark the instant of their rebirth, according to their deeds, in this world or another.

I questioned another lama of the monastery of Labrang, in Amdo, and asked him what he thought would be the condition, in the *bardo*, of a man who had had no belief, religious or other, concerning the after-death, and was convinced that it meant nothingness.

The lama, of course, did not consider that this want of faith was a crime to be punished in the next world, but he doubted whether there existed anyone who had never conceived any idea concerning what would happen after death. As I replied by pointing out that there had been materialists in India (the Charvakas) and that the number of such persons was considerable in the West, he asked me: 'Have these men never, even as children, heard anything taught on the subject of the after-death?' I had to agree that most materialists had received some instruction on the subject. Then, concluded the lama, the descriptions of another world which they have heard, which they have at first believed, and then put aside as absurd, may come back to them and people their *bardo* with visions which reproduce them.

What results from these various theories? Do the Lamaists really believe that one can interfere with the action of Karman during the time which elapses between death and rebirth? Exoterically, at least, they believe it, but they declare that this operation is rarely possible, because its success depends upon the character of the deceased, and upon the degree of knowledge which he has acquired during his lifetime.

The indications furnished by the lama who shows the 'consciousness' which road it should follow in order to reach a certain paradise, or to procure itself a new body, by means of certain virtuous, rich, or intelligent parents, are understood by it only if it has been predisposed to understand them by the actions performed by the dead man. Similarly, the instructions lavished upon it in respect of the mirage, issuing from itself, which stupefies it, cannot be understood by it unless, before death, it has already familiarized itself with those conceptions. All things considered, the law of actions continues to hold good.

Lamaists also tell me that men who, for long periods, have trained themselves to observe and analyse the phenomena which arise in them, and have thus acquired the habit of remaining perfectly conscious, are able to overcome the swoon which tends to supervene at the moment of death, and to avoid it. They thus enter fully conscious into the 'intermediate state', and the phantasmagoria which may occur in it does not occur for them.

These experts in the 'art of dying' have, to a great extent, the power of projecting their consciousness into whatever world they please, and of being reborn in any environment they may select. But this power was already possessed by them, in a latent state, before death; it was the fruit of their psychic training, and thus a result of their deeds (Karman). Moreover, in whatever world and in whatever condition they are reborn, they are in no way protected against the effects of their actions; these effects will occur in a form determined by this world and this condition. The Law of Karman does not act on us from outside; it is in himself that each of us bears the causes of the effects which he experiences.

No teaching *in extremis* or *post mortem* is given to the initiated Lamaist, for he has no need of advice; no rite is celebrated on his account, for he has no need of help; and when his remains are borne to the cemetery no lama holds in his hand the end of a scarf attached thereto, for he has no need of guidance. As a hermit in the Himalayas said to me: 'He knows the road.'

Although the theories concerning the *bardo* have led us deep into Buddhistic heterodoxy, and even, one might say, entirely outside Buddhism, this last picture of the man who knows his road recalls the exhortation addressed to his disciples by the Buddha: 'Be your own torch and your own refuge.' The last word of Tibetan Tantricism is also: 'No one can guide thee but thyself.'

# CHAPTER VII

## NIRVÂNA

IT would seem strange to end a book on Buddhism, however short, without speaking of *Nirvâna*. This expression, among all those associated with Buddhism, is the best known to Westerners. It does not follow from this fact that its meaning is equally clear to them. Quite the contrary. As a rule, the various conceptions of Nirvâna which are current in the West are very far removed from those accepted by Buddhists. I say intentionally 'those' accepted by Buddhists, for Nirvâna has been envisaged by them in more than one way. One may say that in respect of this theme, the subtlety and ingenuity of the Buddhist philosophers have reached their extreme limit. And yet . . . in these many different and even contradictory theories, can we not find a point on which they all agree? It seems that we can. On the other hand, without going into the philosophical minutiae of these theories, can we make a summary classification of them? This too seems to be possible. Let us see.

'Wide open be the door of the Immortal . . .'
(Mahâvagga.)

It was with these words that the Buddha began his

preaching. According to the canonical text, he had just attained illumination while meditating at the foot of a tree beside a river—the Neranjerâ—and what he had realized he at first hesitated to make public. What had he seen and realized? The answer will help us to grasp the conception of Nirvâna held by the authors of this narrative.

'The Venerable One[1] seated himself at the foot of a banyan tree.

'Then, to the mind of the Venerable One, who was alone, who had retired into solitude, this thought presented itself: I have discovered this profound truth, difficult to perceive, difficult to understand, filling the heart with peace, sublime, surpassing all thought, abstruse, to be grasped only by the wise. Struggling in the vortex of the world are men given up to covetousness, tending towards covetousness, finding their pleasure in the world. For men who struggle in the vortex of the world it is a difficult thing to understand the law of causality, the chain of causation; and it will also be extremely difficult to understand the cessation of all formations (samskâras), the rejection of the *upâdhis* (bases of existence), the extinction of desire, the absence of passion, peace of mind, Nirvâna.'

There is a definition of Nirvâna, a definition attributed to the Buddha. Nirvâna is the cessation of the *samskâras*, and these are understood by the Buddhists as being the

---

[1] Bhagavad. A title of respect, given to the Buddha and to certain gods. The hindu *sannyâsins* also employ it among themselves.

'confections' or 'fabrications'. It is ideas that are fabricated; the ideas which we entertain concerning the world and concerning ourselves. As to the bases of existence, they consist of desire, passions, deeds, and the aggregate of the five *skandhas*, i.e. the physical form, the perceptions, the sensations, the mental activity, the consciousness.

To the text quoted above, we may add the following:

'When thou hast understood the dissolution of all the 'fabrications', thou shalt understand that which is not 'fabricated'. (Dhammapada.)

What is it that applies itself to this work of 'fabrication'? It is the mind, using the material provided for it by the perception, the sensations, and the six kinds of consciousness distinguished by the Buddhists, i.e. the consciousness joined to each of the five senses: joined to the eye—consciousness of forms; to the ear—consciousness of sounds; to the nose—consciousness of odours; to the tongue—consciousness of tastes; to the body in general—consciousness of contact through the sense of touch; and, in the sixth place, the consciousness joined to the mind, which means, the consciousness of ideas.

The 'fabrication' of this material is influenced by desire, by the passions, and by deeds, this last expression being understood as meaning the result of the Karman; not only of the individual Karman, but also—and perhaps, *above all*—of the general Karman.[1] Finally, enveloping the whole, is *moha*, 'which soils and spoils that with which

[1] See Chapter VI.

it is mingled'. *Moha* is error, confusion, illusion, the hallucination which prevents the mind from discovering the truth. *Moha* is the antonym of Knowledge (prajñâ) and, 'consequently, is the primordial cause which sets in motion the world-process'.[1] In Buddhism, the world-process is the Chain of Interdependent Origins, which we can sum up in three points, as did the great Mahâyânist philosopher Nagârjuna: ignorance, desire, action.[2] *Moha* is ignorance (*avidyâ*) in the form which it assumes in each of us. On account of our mental confusion, and the illusion which leads us to conceive wrong notions and form wrong judgements, the data furnished by our senses, perceptions, and sensations are faulty; passions and desire arise within us, and these engender the accomplishment of evil deeds. All actions, even the most virtuous, are regarded as evil, that is, as productive of unhappy results, so long as any error is involved in them.

If, then, in the last resort, that which constitutes the *samsâra* (the round of phenomena, the world) is ignorance, desire, and action, it goes without saying that Nirvâna, the opposite of *samsâra*, must be the absence of ignorance, desire, and action. What action? Forming wrong ideas under the influence of ignorance and desire. A very definite statement of Candrakîrti leaves no room for doubt on this point: 'The essence of Nirvâna consists simply in the suppression of all the constructions of our fertile imagination.'[3]

[1] Stcherbatsky: *The Central Conception of Buddhism.*    [2] See Chapter IV.
[3] Candrakîrti, *Commentary on the Madyamika-çastra of Nagârjuna.*

According to an opinion which is widely held in the West, Nirvâna consists in the annihilation of the soul after death. This opinion is totally erroneous. Buddhism denies the existence of an 'ego', of a soul, or of any permanent principle whatsoever;[1] this denial constitutes one of its fundamental doctrines, so how could it consider and teach the annihilation of something which, according to the formal declarations attributed to the Buddha, does not exist?

Whether we can understand Nothingness, Absolute Non-entity, is doubtful; behind the thing that disappears we cannot help imagining something else. As for India, there a beginning is always regarded as the beginning of something arising from something else, and an end is regarded as the end of something which is transformed into something else, or is united with something else. Aryan thinkers have long repeated that 'that which is not cannot come into existence, and that which is cannot cease to be'. Is this theory in contradiction with that of the momentariness of the elements? The Buddhists say not, for existence, which is activity, links action to action in a perpetual becoming.

The meaning of the word Nirvâna is, without a doubt, the cause of the erroneous opinion which Westerners have conceived as to the nature of Nirvâna. Nirvâna means an extinction, or rather, the action of a breath which blows upon a flame and extinguishes it. Extinction,

[1] See Chapter V.

therefore nothingness, so runs the argument. The question
is: what, according to the Buddhists, is extinguished? This
is what they reply:

A Brahmin ascetic questioned Sâriputra, an eminent
disciple of the Buddha:

'Nirvâna, Nirvâna, they say, friend Sâriputra. What
then is Nirvâna?'

'The annihilation of desire, the annihilation of hatred,
the annihilation of error (*moha*), that, friend, is what is
called Nirvâna.' (Samyutta Nikâya.)

'By what abandonment does Nirvâna exist?' asks
Udaya of the Buddha.

'By the abandonment of desire Nirvâna exists.'
(Sutta Nipâta.)

'By the rejection of covetousness, of ill-will, and of all
error shalt thou attain Nirvâna.' (Mahâ Parinibbâna sutta.)

'In this world much has been seen, heard, and thought;
the destruction of passion and of desire for the objects
which have been perceived is this imperishable Nirvâna.'
(Samyutta Nikâya.)

'Those who are detached, in this world, from all that
has been seen, heard, or thought,[1] from all virtue and
from all works; those who, after having become detached
from all kinds of things, and having understood the
essence of desire, are without passions, those I call men
who have crossed the river." (Sutta Nipâta.)

[1] We may liken 'that which has been seen, heard and thought' to the
'habit-energy' or 'memory' (*vâsanâ*), a Mahâyânist conception which is
mentioned in the following pages.

'To cross the river' or 'to reach the other shore' are classic expressions in Buddhist literature, and mean, to attain Nirvâna.

Elsewhere, also, there is mention of 'the disciple who has rejected pleasure and desire, and who has attained, even in this world, to Deliverance from death, to repose, Nirvâna, the eternal home.' (Suttasangaga.)

The Hinâyânists, at least in their ancient sect of the Sarvastivâdins, believed in the reality of the material world, consisting in a continual *becoming* (*bhava*). Thus Nirvâna was equivalent to the cessation of the activity which maintained the existence (the continual 'becoming') of the series (*santâna*) of successive moments of consciousness which constitutes that which we regard as our 'I'. Is this cessation of the series of successive moments of consciousness, or this cessation of all 'formations', equivalent to nonentity?—Nothing of the kind has ever been declared.

We are told in the *Majjhihima Nikâya* that this question was definitely put to the Buddha by Malunkyâputta: 'After death, does a Buddha (he who has attained Nirvâna) exist, or does he not exist?' The Buddha did not reply, but he explained the reason for his silence on this point. A reply to this question would be profitless for him who received it, said the Buddha. 'Whether the Buddha exists or does not exist after death, one fact remains: there is birth, decrepitude, death, suffering, on which subjects I have given my teachings, showing the origin, the cause, and the ending of suffering, and the Way which leads to

this ending . . . I have not said whether the Buddha exists
or does not exist after death because that has nothing to
do with the foundations of the doctrine and does not
lead to the absence of passion, to peace, to supernormal
faculties, to the supreme wisdom, to Nirvâna.'

Why did the Buddha not answer? A Mahâyânist
cannot help thinking that Malunkyâputta's question dealt
with a false conception, that of the duality of being and
not-being. Had not the Buddha declared that 'for him
who knows according to the reality, there is neither
being, nor not-being?' Had he not also said that he re-
pudiated the two opposing theories of the annihilation
and of the eternal life of an *ego*? All such theories are
'fabrications' of our mind, dominated by error, illusion,
and wrong ideas (*moha*) which vitiate our reasoning.
The Buddha neither exists nor ceases to exist after death,
in the way in which our ignorance leads us to imagine
those two states, and never did he exist during that which
we call *his life*, in the meaning which our ignorance gives
to the word *exist*. It is the same with us, who do not exist
in the way in which we imagine ourselves to exist, for
'nothing is born, nothing dies; nothing comes, nothing
goes', said Nâgârjuna, the founder of the Mâhâyana,
and all the theories of survival or annihilation which we
evolve have their basis in the illusion of duality by which
we are possessed; they are 'constructions of our fertile
imagination.'[1]

The old-time Buddhists seem to have been very deeply

[1] Candrakîrti. Quoted above.

impressed by the spectacle of the ills inherent in life, and their conception of Nirvâna is, above all, that of the ending of these sufferings. We find in the *Questions of King Milinda* a series of parables by which Nagâsêna sought to explain to the Greek prince Menander the natura of Nirvâna. Here are some of them.

'Nirvâna, so full of peace, of happiness, so subtle, exists, O King. He who regulates his life correctly, understanding the nature of the formations (or fabrications; the *samskâras*) according to the teachings of the Buddhas, realizes it by his wisdom, as an apprentice, following the instructions of his master, makes himself a master of his craft.

'And if thou shouldst ask: "How may Nirvâna be known?" It is by deliverance from distress and from danger, by peace, calm, happiness, contentment, purity.

'Just as a man, O King, who had fallen into a blazing furnace filled with many faggots of dry wood, if by a great effort he saved himself and reached a cool place, he would feel the greatest happiness—so is it with whoever rules his life rightly. Such a one, by his attentive reflection, realizes the supreme felicity of Nirvâna, where the burning heat of the triple fire (sensuality-covetousness; hate-malice; error-stupidity) is entirely extinguished. The furnace represents the triple fire, as the man who was burning therein, and who escaped, represents him who guides his life aright, and as the cool place stands for Nirvâna.

'Again, as a man who had fallen into a trench filled

with corpses and filth, if he succeeded in getting out and reaching a place free from corpses, would feel supremely happy, so is it with whoever guides his life aright. Such a one, by attentive reflection, will realize the supreme felicity of Nirvâna, from which the corpses of all evil propensities have been removed.

'Again, as a man who had fallen amongst foes, trembling with fear, confused and troubled in mind, if by a great effort he succeeded in freeing himself, and fled to a place where he was perfectly safe, he would feel supremely happy, so is it with whoever orders his life aright. Such a one, by attentive reflection, will realize the supreme bliss of Nirvâna from which fear and terror are banished.

'The terror, O King, represents this ceaselessly renewed anxiety in respect of birth, decrepitude, illness and death, and the place of refuge represents Nirvâna.

'Again, as a man who has fallen into a place full of filth, of mud and slime, if, by a violent effort, he frees himself from the mud and slime and reaches a clean place, one without foulness, he will feel great happiness, so also whoever regulates aright his life, will, by attentive reflection, acquire the supreme bliss of Nirvâna, from which the mud and slime of evil propensities have been expelled. The mud and slime, O King, represent riches, honours, eulogies[1] and the clean place represents Nirvâna.

[1] Compare the following passage, taken from the *Sûtra in Forty-two Articles*. 'In the eyes of the Tathâgata (the Buddha) all the most perfect splendours of kings and of their ministers are as spittle and dust.

'In his eyes, gold, silver, and all other jewels or precious objects are as brick and gravel.'

'And again, if one should ask: How does he who guides his life aright realize Nirvâna? I should answer: He, O King, grasps the truth concerning the development of the "formations" (samskâras), and then perceives, in this development, birth, decay, illness, death, but he does not, in this development, perceive either happiness or contentment; he sees in it nothing which is worth holding on to.

'And discontent arises in his mind, since he finds nothing on which he can rest and which is sure to give him a lasting satisfaction. He becomes impatient, and without refuge, without protection, without hope, he tires of these reiterated lives.' (The continual round of deaths and births.)

'And in the mind of him who thus perceives the insecurity of life, ceaselessly recommencing, this thought arises: All is on fire, blazing and burning[1] in this endless renewal. It is full of suffering, full of despair. If, he thinks, one could attain to a state in which there is no more "becoming", there would be calm, tranquillity, the ending of the "fabrications", the liberation of the essential bases of life (upadha), the ending of cupidity, the absence of passion: peace, Nirvâna. And then his mind strives toward this state where there is no "becoming"; and then he has found peace, then he triumphs and rejoices in this thought: At last I have attained a refuge.

---

[1] This allegory of the flame is frequently used in the Buddhist Scriptures: 'Everything burns, O disciples. . . . With what fire is it burning? I declare to you, it is with the fire of thirst (desire-covetousness). With the fire of hatred, with the fire of ignorance.' (Mahâvagga.)

'Just as a man who has adventured into a foreign country and has lost his way, when he knows of a path free from jungle which leads to his home, will hasten along his path, glad of mind, exulting and rejoicing in this thought: "At last I have found the road": so he who has perceived the insecurity of life . . . (the text continues as above) . . . "At last I have attained a refuge." And he struggles with all his strength along this path, so that he shall be firm in his effort, so that he shall remain constant in love toward all beings in all the worlds, and so he continues always to apply himself, until, passing beyond the impermanent, he attains Reality. And when he has attained that, O King, the man who has ordered his life aright has understood Nirvâna and sees it face to face.'[1]

A Refuge, or Place of Peace, Nirvâna is not, however, a particular spot; Nâgasêna is careful to warn his royal questioner of this.

'Venerable Nâgasêna,' asks the prince, 'is there a place where Nirvâna is situated?'

'There is no place, O King, where Nirvâna is situated. . . . It is the same with fire, which exists without there being a place where fire is situated. But if a man rubs two sticks one against the other, fire is produced; so also, although it is not situated anywhere, Nirvâna exists, and by means of vigilant attention, in no matter what country, in the dwelling of the Nâgas (divinities of the Ocean) or in the highest Paradise, he who rules his life aright will attain Nirvâna.

[1] Abridged from the *Questions of King Milinda*.

'Just as a man who has eyes, no matter where he may be, is able to contemplate the vault of the sky, and to see before him the horizon, so he who lives with uprightness and vigilant attention, in whatever place he may be, will attain Nirvâna.'

From the above one may deduce that Nâgasêna regarded Nirvâna as the cessation of the evils inherent in existence, inherent in the rotation of the Wheel or endless Chain of Interdependent Origins, and that this cessation occurred, not because one passed on to another world, but because one had induced, by the practice of virtue and vigilant attention, a particular spiritual state.

As I said at the beginning of this chapter, the question of Nirvâna has given rise, among Buddhists, to many theories, of which a certain number are concerned with the reality or non-reality of *samsâra* and Nirvâna. It must always be borne in mind that in these discussions, among Buddhists, unreal or non-real does not mean exactly: 'which does not exist', but signifies rather: 'which is produced by causes'; therefore, that which has no proper nature, is not autogenous. This has been explained in Chapter V.

It is thus that the reality of the 'ego' is denied; not that the person does not *exist*, but because it is an aggregation of various elements which can be perceived, distinguished, and named separately.

Up to a certain point, and perhaps not with complete unanimity, the modern Theravadins share the views of

the ancient Hinâyânists, who believed in the reality of
the material world. According to them, also, Nirvâna
consists in the definite cessation of the 'becoming', of
the series (*santâna*) of successive moments of consciousness, which we wrongly imagine to be our 'self'. As I
noted in Chapter VI, this 'series', which continues through
successive deaths and rebirths, is, although the Theravadins
deny it, a disguised 'ego'.[1] Popular Buddhism, with its
tales of successive lives of the same individual, has never
failed to understand it thus, and does not in any way differ,
on this point, from Brahmanism, which teaches the
reincarnation of an 'ego' (jîva).

Nirvâna—the individual Nirvâna—as the Maha Thera
Nyanâtiloka[2] once orally explained to me, consists in
the suppression, the extinction of *one* series (*santâna*). As
to the other 'series', he appeared to see them continuing,
through successive deaths and rebirths, until, one by
one, they in their turn came to cease.

Among the ancient Hinâyânists there were also some
who believed that all the elements, all the energies whose
activities constitute the world, could in the course of time
enter into a final state of rest, and it seems that they
pictured to themselves, in this way, a general Nirvâna.
Nevertheless, this Nirvâna was considered a real thing
(perhaps an element: *Dharma*) although inert. In this

[1] On the other hand, there have existed Buddhist sects which taught the
temporary continuity of the individuality of 'person': the *pudgala*. Nevertheless, they did not look upon it as an 'ego', as the *pudgala* was said to be
impermanent.

[2] A German Orientalist who is a Buddhist *bhikkhu*, and the head of a group
of European Buddhist *bhikkhus*, established in Ceylon for the past thirty years.

connection, a Buddhist *bhikkhu*, a native of India, the Reverend Kâli Kumar, told me that if this Nirvâna were real, and if it were a *thing*—whatever special sense one may give to these terms—it could not for ever remain inactive.

The speaker did not admit that existence could become non-existence; something which had existed must, in one form or another, exist for ever. In his opinion a Nirvâna of this kind offered some analogy to the *pralâya* of the Brahmanists. (The destruction of the universe at the end of a *kalpa*, a period of time comprising 1,000 yugas or 432 millions of our years, and corresponding to one 'day of Brahma.') According to this conception, the universe, or the manifestation of Brahma, is emitted at the beginning of the 'day of Brahma', and it returns into Brahma for another period of time called the 'night of Brahma', during which there is no manifestation. The alternations of manifestation and non-manifestation are thus represented as following the rhythm of the breathing of Brahma, the exhalation causing the world to arise with the breath, and the inhalation causing it to return to Brahma.

According to another Brahminic theory, the state of non-manifestation corresponds to the equilibrium of the three *gunas* (qualities), to wit: *sattva*, goodness-purity; *rajas*, energy-activity; *tamas*, torpor-stupidity. The manifestation, that is to say, the phenomenon, is produced by the predominance of one or the other quality; by the varied proportion of these qualities. When a perfect equality of proportion is re-established, the movement of the phenomenon ceases, only to start afresh when the equilibrium of the three qualities is again disturbed, at the end of the 'night of Brahma.'

In the same way, thought the Reverend Kâli Kumar, a Nirvâna consisting in the extinction of the *series* of successive moments of consciousness (*santâna*) or in the extinction of anything that had existed, could not be eternal, because it was produced by causes, and nothing which is produced by causes can be permanent or real.

And if this Nirvâna, deprived of life and activity, were a thing, a substance, an entity existing by itself, and not produced, it could have no relation to us, for if the activity of our five *skandhas* (physical form—perception—sensation—mental activity—consciousness) were extinguished in this inert reality, this fact would change the nature of it, would impart into it a cause apt to awaken movement in it.

I do not know what retort his predecessors in the Order who had conceived this special sort of Nirvâna would have made to my reverend friend, supposing that they had really conceived such a theory, and that we are not mistaken as to their thought.

A clear line of demarcation between the Hinâyânist idea of Nirvâna and that which is current among Mahâyânists is traced by the fact that as we have just seen, in their different conceptions of Nirvâna, the Hinâyânists always regard it as different from, and even the opposite of, *samsâra*. The comparison, familiar among them, of the crossing to the 'other bank' of a river which separates this 'other bank' (Nirvâna) from that on which we find ourselves (*samsâra*), corresponds exactly to this conception. The Mahâyânists, on the other hand, proclaim that Nirvâna and *samsâra* are one and the same thing. Seen from one angle, it is *samsâra*; seen from another, it is Nirvâna.

The basis of this doctrine is seen to be perfectly orthodox, if we consider the definition of the Chain of Interdependent Origins, where ignorance is declared to be the cause that sets in motion the round of phenomena with the 'mass of suffering' that goes with them. The suppression of ignorance brings about the suppression of the 'round' (*samsâra*), and it is this suppression which constitutes Nirvâna. Now, what the Mahâyânists declare is just this: that what appears as *samsâra* to the ignorant appears as Nirvâna to him who is enlightened.

'Between Nirvâna and *samsâra*,' says Candrakîrti, 'there is not the slightest difference.' It must be understood that in Nirvâna nothing is suppressed, nothing is destroyed in reality. Nirvâna simply consists in the complete suppression of all the false constructions of our imagination. As declared by the Buddha, the real, fundamental elements of existence can never be destroyed. The things which do not exist in this world do not exist and have never existed. Those who imagine existence and non-existence (as a duality of opposites) will never understand the rest from *samsâra* (from the world of phenomena).

The meaning of this is as follows: In the Absolute, which is the final Nirvâna, all the elements have disappeared. Whether they be called stains (*klesha*) or generative power (*karman*) or individual existence, or groups of elements, all have completely disappeared. But these elements which do not exist in the Absolute have never existed. They resemble the rope which a man sees in the darkness, and takes for a snake; as soon as one brings a lamp, the man sees his mistake, and the fear with which the rope inspired him is dispelled. The elements called illusion, desire, karma, and birth, which constitute the individual life, have no real existence in the absolute meaning of this word; they have none even in the restricted sense as regards the conditions of life in *samsâra*. The rope which was taken for a snake is not in itself a snake, nor is it ever a snake, either in the darkness or in the light.

'What is it, then, that is called phenomenal reality (*samsâra*)? Obsessed by the unreal demons of their 'ego' and of their 'mine', stupid people—those who are of the world[1]—imagine that they can perceive separate entities, whereas in reality these do not exist; just as a man suffering from an eye disease may see in front of him hairs, flies, or other objects which do not exist.

Consequently, it has been said:

'Nirvâna is not non-existence;
'How could you have this idea?

---

[1] Those who live an ordinary life: *prithag jana*, in contradistinction to the enlightened man, the *arya* (the noble) who has entered the paths 'beyond the world'.

'We call Nirvâna the cessation
'Of all thoughts of non-existence and of existence.'[1]

The Hinâyânist theory which distinguishes two kinds
of Nirvâna: (1) Nirvâna in this life, consisting in spiritual
illumination, suppression of illusion-error, desire, and
hatred; and (2) *Parinirvâna*, attained after death, which
consists in the extinction of the *skandhas* (the body—the
perceptions—the sensations—mental activity—consciousness), may be held to be one of the effects of the belief
in the duality of *samsâra* and Nirvâna. This conception
tends to give death an importance which it loses alto-
gether in the Mahâyânist doctrine of the unreality of the
world. The distinction made between the condition which
exists during the duration of a group of elements forming
a living individual, and the state produced by the suppression of this group, after the death of this individual,
also gives this group a character of 'temporary permanence'. Though it is limited to the length of the life
of the individual, this supposed permanency disagrees
with the Buddhist doctrine which states that the components which form the 'group' are continually renewed,
and that the life of an individual lasts only 'as long as a
thought' or 'as long as a breath'. If so, the end of the group
occurs at every moment, in the sense that the present group
is not identical with that which preceded it, while the
future group is not identical with the present one. As for

[1] Abridged from Candrakîrti's *Commentary on Nâgârjuna's Treatise on
Relativity*, translated by Stcherbatsky.

an 'extinction of the *skandhas*', this can have no meaning
apart from the belief in a purely individual life. The fact
of the continual exchanges which are going on between
the various groups or 'series' (*santâna*), as well as the fact
of the uninterrupted transit through the world of energies
continually engendered by the universal activity, excludes
all idea of a cessation, a halt, or any sort of end.

The position of the Mahâyânist thinkers is stronger,
and, undoubtedly, actually more in conformity with the
spirit of Buddhism, when they declare that the world,
such as we conceive it, is an effect of our imagination.
So declaring, they have not to defend any theories concerning this world and our personality as we see them,
since they state, at the outset, that our ignorance, our
mental blindness, erects a deceptive mirage between us
and Reality.

Nirvâna, in this case, is neither to reach 'the other shore'
nor to die and sink into the nothingness of the absolute
ending of all the elements of life. It is simply the awakening from an unpleasant dream, the ending of a mental
illness; it is to *see aright*.

'There is only one kind of Nirvâna,' it is said in the
*Lotus of the Good Law*, a work in great renown among
Japanese Buddhists. And this Nirvâna is shown, in the
same work, as being attained by him who has recognized
that 'all phenomena are a sort of mirage, a sort of
dream'; that they are devoid of proper essence (individual
nature).

Nirvâna becomes, for the Mahâyânist, a synonym of Reality, designated also by the term 'Void'.

'Void' must never be taken in the sense of Nothingness or of nonentity.

Void means: void of all the imaginary qualities which we superimpose on reality; void of duality. This is what Nâgârjuna says in the following strophe, which serves as an introduction to several of his works, and which expresses the fundamental idea of the Mâhâyana.

'I pay homage to this perfectly enlightened Buddha, who has taught the doctrine of Interdependent Origins, according to which there is neither cessation nor production (birth); neither impermanence nor permanence; neither difference nor identity; and which calms activity (that which 'fabricates' chimerical conceptions).'

We read in the *Lankavatara sûtra*:

'That which is meant by the *Void*, in the highest sense of ultimate Reality, is that in the acquisition of an inner understanding, by means of wisdom, there is no trace of "the force of habit" (memory) caused by erroneous conceptions (which have been produced) during a past which had no beginning.'

It must be understood that the familiar term 'force of habit' which is used here excludes the idea of an energy produced by, but differing from, habit. It is the habit itself which is the force. And this habit is identical with memory (vasâna).

And what is the meaning of 'things are not born'?

'When it is said "nothing is born", that does not mean that things are not born; it means that they are not self-produced. In a profound sense, to be without any self-nature is equivalent to not being born. That all things are without self-nature means that there is a continual and uninterrupted "becoming", a changing, every moment, from one state of "existence" to another.

'And what does non-duality mean? It means that light and shade, long and short, black and white, are relative terms which depend on one another. Nirvâna and *samsâra* are *not two*, and it is the same with all things.

'There is no Nirvâna except where there is *samsâra*; there is no *samsâra* except where there is Nirvâna.'

This identity is constantly affirmed in all Mahâyânist works.

In the *Prajñâ Pâramita Hridaya sûtra* the identity of the *skandhas* with the Void—that is to say with Nirvâna—is clearly stated:

'There are five *skandhas*, and these should be regarded as being void by nature. Form (the body) is void, and the void is really form. The void is not different from the form, and the form is not different from the void. That which is form, that is the void; that which is void, that is the form.' In the larger version of the *Prajñâ Pâramita* it is added: 'Apart from form there is no void, apart from the void there is no form.'

The same thing is repeated in respect of the four other *skandhas*, which form the mental part of the group known as an individual; that is to say: perceptions, sensations, mental fabrications, and consciousness.

In less scholastic phrasing, this amounts to saying: Nirvâna is just *samsâra*; the individual, formed of the five *skandhas*, such as he is, *is* the Void, Reality, Nirvâna.

'Neither birth, nor annihilation, that is what I call Nirvâna. Nirvâna means the perception of reality, much as it really is in itself. And when, by the effect of a complete change of all the mental processes,[1] there comes the acquisition of understanding of oneself (and by oneself) that I call Nirvâna.' (Lankavatara sûtra.)

It is this reversal of the notions to which we adhere under the influence of the 'force of habit' that the spiritual Masters belonging to the sect of meditation (Ts'an in China and Zen in Japan) endeavour to produce in their disciples by means of the enigmas (called *Koan*) which they set them.

This 'force of habit' (or memory) should be understood as the totality of mental formations or 'confections' (ideas, conceptions) which have been produced in the course of a past without beginning. It is this 'force of habit' that creates the mirage of the world, and which creates it afresh at each moment, with the contribution that we provide for it by our mental activity, acting in the sense

---

[1] *Paravritti*, a kind of mental revolution which causes all things to be seen in a different manner, and causes contact to be made with them by new means. The exact meaning of *paravritti* is 'turning back', 'upsetting'.

of this habit. When it is said that *samsâra* is a product of 'our constructive imagination', we should not take this as meaning that a single individual, or group of *skandhas*, alone, can cause *samsâra* to emerge. It should be understood that the energy begotten by false reasoning and wrong ideas, during 'a past without beginning', has produced this mirage, which our adhesion helps to perpetuate.

The consciousness of ideas, which supplements the consciousness attached to the senses (to the eye, the consciousness of form, etc.) 'distinguishes an objective world, and is thus kept in motion (produces new ideas concerning that which it perceives). It attaches itself to this objective world, and by the effect of manifold "forces of habit" it nourishes the Alaya Vijnâna (the depository of consciousness).' (Lankavatara sûtra.)

In this 'reservoir' or 'depository' are also the germs of ideas that weave the veil of illusion of *samsâra* in our mind. These germs are ancient conceptions, which, having become memory or 'force of habit'—universal memory, as has just been said—operate, unknown to us, in our subconscious mind.

Thus the entire drama of *samsâra* and Nirvâna is played in the mind, for Nirvâna and *samsâra*, and all the theories about them, are nothing but products of our 'productive imagination'. Does this mean that the world has no existence, that we do not exist? Not at all. Both the world and we ourselves exist, but neither exists in itself, neither is self-generated; both are 'products', or 'caused'; and there-

fore Tsong Khapa and his disciples declare them to be
unreal, for they are made of the substance of others.

Moreover, we do not perceive *samsâra* as it is in reality.
Our 'productive imagination' fed by 'the energy engendered by habit', during 'a past without beginning',
superimposes on the reality an illusory form, 'a mirage',
'images such as those seen in a dream'. (Vajracchedika
sûtra.) The cessation of this constructive activity, the
awakening from the dream, is Nirvâna.

In conclusion, it is interesting to note that Tibetan
Buddhists have no word which translates the exact
meaning of the term Nirvâna: the extinction of a flame
by blowing it out. It is not because they were unable to
express this idea in their language. The translators of the
canonical Sanskrit scriptures, whether Tibetans or
Indians who had come to Tibet as missionaries, had a
perfect knowledge of both languages, as is shown by
every page of their translation. Nirvâna, however, was
left untranslated.

The expressions used by the Tibetans are: *nya nien les
despa*,[1] literally 'gone beyond misery or suffering'. But
this expression is also currently used to say, in polite
language, that someone is dead. It is equivalent to the
phrase *Shing la peb song*,[2] 'he has gone to the sphere of
the Buddha', which is employed when speaking respectfully of the death of a lama.

The real terms for Nirvâna are: *tharpa*, 'liberation,'

---

[1] Written: *nya ngan las hdas pa.*          [2] Written: *shing la pheb song.*

and *sangyais-o*,[1] 'become Buddha'; *tharpa* being the more commonly used of the two.

There is not a Tibetan who doubts the possibility of attaining this liberation, and becoming a Buddha in our present life. There even exists in Tibet a mystical doctrine known as the 'short path' (*lam chung*) of which the aim is to lead its followers rapidly to liberation. The first spiritual guide of the famous poet-ascetic, Milarespa, told him: 'The doctrine which I teach is such that he who meditates on it during the day attains liberation during the following night, and he who meditates on it during the night attains liberation during the following day.'

It concerns a method supposed to be capable of bringing about a sudden change of perceptions and ideas, a change analogous to *satori*, from which the Japanese followers of the Zen Sect also expect the revelation of Reality, 'impossible to know from the exterior, impossible to understand by reasoning, and non-duality', which is always present about us and in us, and which our 'constructive imagination' divides, wrongly, into *samsâra* and Nirvâna.

'It is not a duality, it must not be divided into two,' is repeated many times in the *Prajñâ Pâramita*, and this may well be the last word of Mahâyânist philosophy concerning Nirvâna.

[1] Written: *sangs rgyas ho.*

# APPENDICES

# SIJALOVADA SUTTA

## MORAL RULES FOR LAYMEN

THUS have I heard:

At that time the Buddha was staying near Râjagaha, in the park that is called Veluvana.

One day the young householder Sijâla, having risen early, went out from the city, and standing upright, his hair and his garments dripping with water, raising his clasped hands above his head, he bowed in adoration to the cardinal points: to the East, to the South, to the West, to the North, to the Nadir, and to the Zenith.

However, the Buddha, having risen early, clothed himself, and, carrying his begging bowl, set out for Râjagaha, there to beg his food. On his way, seeing Sijâla with his clothes and his hair wet, raising his clasped hands toward the sky, and bowing down in the direction of the cardinal points, the Venerable One questioned him:

'Why then, O young man, hast thou risen at this early hour, and why, leaving Râjagaha, dost thou stand here with wet hair and clothes, bowing down to the cardinal points?'

'Master, my father, on his death-bed, said to me: "My

son, never neglect to pay reverence to the cardinal points.''
Thus, filled with respect and veneration for his words,
holding them as sacred, I go out from the city in the early
morning to adore the East, the South, the West, the
North, the Nadir and the Zenith.'

'It is not thus, O young man, that the Sages teach that
the cardinal points should be revered.'

'How then, O Master, ought one to revere them? Deign
to enlighten me, that I may know the teaching of the
Sages.'

'Give ear then, young man, pay attention to my words.
I will instruct thee.'

'So be it,' replied Sijâla.

And the Buddha spoke:

'Young man, the disciple of the Sages has rejected the
four defilements, the four tendencies leading to evil
have ceased to control him, he has avoided the six ways
of dissipating his wealth, and thus, freed from the
fourteen evils and keeping watch on the cardinal points,
he strides, victorious, through the worlds. For him, this
world and the other worlds are equally blessed, and he
will be reborn in a heavenly realm.

'What are the four defilements?

'To take life is a defilement.
'To take that which has not been given is a
      defilement.
'Impurity is a defilement.
'Lying is a defilement.

'These four defilements are rejected by him who leads a holy life.

'What are the harmful qualities that lead men to evil?

'Partiality leads men to do evil.
'Anger leads men to do evil.
'Ignorance leads men to do evil.
'Fear leads men to do evil.

'Partiality, anger, ignorance and fear having ceased to influence the disciple of the Sages, these harmful tendencies can no longer lead him to do evil.

'The fame of him who through partiality, anger, ignorance or fear swerves from justice, will pass and will decline like the waning moon; but the glory of him who, being freed from those obstacles, remains faithful to justice, will grow like the splendour of the waxing moon.

'What are the ways of dissipating wealth?

'Intemperance.
'Love of the theatre and of feasts.
'Evil companions.
'Gambling.
'Idleness.
'The habit of spending the night wandering about the town.

'These six things lead a man to poverty.

'Six evils, young man, are bound up with intemperance: poverty, quarrels, illnesses, degradation of character, scandal, and the weakening of the faculties.

'Six evils wait for him who wanders in the town at night: His life is in danger, his wife and children are left unprotected, his property is not guarded; he is suspected of frequenting places of ill-fame, evil gossip circulates about him, sorrow and remorse follow him.

'Six evils are the lot of him who is dominated by the passion for worldly pleasures. His life is wholly absorbed by the preoccupation of knowing where there will be dancing, where there will be singing, where there will be music, where there will be recitations, where there will be acrobats, where there will be something to see.

'Six evils lie in wait for the gambler. If he wins he is a prey to animosity, if he loses he is assailed by grief. He wastes his fortune. Before the magistrates his word is valueless. His friends and relations scorn him. He is considered unfit for marriage, for according to the common saying: "The gambler is incapable of providing for the needs of a wife."

'Six evils are the lot of him who frequents bad companions. For his friends he has only gamblers, rakes, tricksters, rogues, and outlaws.

'Six evils wait for him who is indolent. He says: It is too cold to work, it is too hot to work, it is too soon to work, it is too late to work. I am hungry and cannot work. I have eaten too much and cannot work, and while his life passes in this way, neglecting his duties, he does not acquire new property and loses the property which he possessed.

'Some friends are only boon companions, some are false. The real friend is he who is still faithful when we have need of him.

'Sleeping late after the sun has risen, committing adultery, being vindictive, spiteful, avaricious, keeping bad company, these six things lead a man to destruction.

'He who takes as his companions men given up to evil, he who commits evil actions, will be lost in this world and in other worlds.

'Gambling, debauchery, love of dancing, of singing (feasts), sleeping by day and wandering by night, evil company and avarice, these six things lead a man to this ruin.

'Unhappy is the gambler, the drunkard, he who has guilty relations with the wife of another, who follows the wicked and honours not the Sages; he will waste like the waning moon.

'He who abandons himself to intoxicating drinks becomes needy and miserable; for ever burning with an insatiable thirst, he drowns in debts as others drown in water, and plunges his family into distress.

'He who sleeps by day and wanders by night in the town, who is always full of drink and given up to debauchery, is incapable of supporting a family.

'Poverty will fasten upon him who says: it is too hot, it is too cold, and thus neglects his daily duty; but he who does his duty as a man, caring not a straw for the cold and the heat, that man will assure his happiness.

'Of four kinds are those who, appearing to be our friends, are only disguised enemies. They are friends from interest, good-for-nothings, flatterers and rakes.

'In four ways the friend from interest shows himself a false friend. He enriches himself at your expense; he exacts much and gives little in return; he acts equitably only when constrained by fear, and he helps you only from selfish motives.

'In four ways the good-for-nothing shows himself a false friend. He boasts of what he would have liked to do for you; he boasts of what he would like to do for you; he abounds with compliments, but when you ask for his services he excuses himself, pretending that it is impossible for him to help you.

'In four ways the flatterer shows himself a false friend. He agrees with you when you do wrong, he agrees with you when you do right; he praises you to your face and speaks ill of you behind your back.

'In four ways the rake shows himself a false friend. He is your companion when it is a question of drinking, of strolling about the town at night, of entering the haunts of pleasure or the gambling houses.

'Knowing for what they are: the interested friends, the disloyal friends, the flatterers, and those who are only companions in debauchery, the wise man avoids them as he would a road planted with ambushes.

'The true friend, young man, is the vigilant friend, he

whose feelings towards you remain the same in prosperity and in adversity, he who gives you good counsel, he who surrounds you with his sympathy.

'In four ways the vigilant friend shows himself a real friend. He watches over you when you are defenceless; he oversees your property when you are negligent; he offers you asylum in time of danger, and when he can he procures you the means of increasing your fortune.

'In four ways he whose sentiments towards you remain the same in prosperity and in adversity shows himself a real friend. He confides to you his secrets and faithfully guards yours; he does not abandon you when you are in trouble, and he would lay down his life to save yours.

'In four ways the giver of good counsel shows himself a real friend. He combats your vices, he encourages you to virtue, he instructs you, he shows you the way leading to the higher worlds.

'In four ways he who surrounds you with his sympathy shows himself a real friend. He shares your sorrows, he rejoices in your joys, he intervenes to silence those who speak ill of you, he applauds those who speak well of you.

'Discerning the true friends, the vigilant friend, the faithful friend, the good counsellor, and he who surrounds you with his sympathy, the wise man will cling to them as a mother clings to her young son.

'With a light like that of a blazing fire shines the sage who holds fast to justice.

'Even as the ant's nest grows higher little by little, even so accumulate the riches of the man who amasses his property as the bees amass their honey. Acquiring his riches in this way, he brings no reproach upon his family.

'Let him divide that which belongs to him into four parts. One part will serve for his upkeep, two other parts will be devoted to his business; let him then save the fourth, so that he can lay his hands on it in case of ill-fortune.

'How does the disciple of the Sages reverence the cardinal points?

'Know first, young man, what the cardinal points represent. The East represents parents, the South teachers, the West wife and children, the North friends, the Zenith spiritual masters, the Nadir servants and those dependent on us.

'A son shows in five ways his veneration for his parents: He satisfies their wants as they satisfied his; he replaces them in the duties which fall to them, he makes himself worthy to become their heir; he watches over their possessions; and when they are dead he respectfully cherishes their memory.

'Parents show in five ways their love for their children: They preserve them from vice, they give them a good education, they marry them honourably, and, at the right time, they give them their family inheritance.

'The pupil honours his teachers in five ways. By rising in their presence, by serving them, by obeying them, by supplying their wants, by being attentive to their teaching.

'The master shows in five ways his affection for his pupils. He trains them in all that is good, he teaches them to cherish knowledge, he instructs them in the sciences and in various subjects, he speaks well of them, and he protects them if they are in danger.

'The husband shows in five ways his love for his wife. He treats her with respect, and with kindness, he is faithful to her, he takes care that she is honoured by others, he provides suitably for her needs.

'The wife shows in five ways her love for her husband. She directs her house in orderly fashion, she receives hospitably the family and friends of her husband, she is chaste, she is a capable housewife, and she zealously and deftly performs the duties which are incumbent on her.

'A man shows his feelings of friendship in five ways. By being generous, affable, and kindly, by acting towards others as he would wish them to act towards him, by sharing with his friends the property which he enjoys.

'In five ways also one should respond to this conduct on the part of a friend. By watching over him when he is not on his guard, by watching over his property when he is neglectful, by offering him asylum in case of danger, by not abandoning him in misfortune, by showing kindness to and interest in his family.

'The master should promote in five ways the well-being of his servants. By suiting their work to their strength, by giving them suitable food and wages, by caring for them when ill, by sharing delicacies with them on exceptional occasions of domestic rejoicing, by allowing them leisure.

'In five ways also servants should respond to this conduct on the part of their master. By rising earlier than he does, by retiring later to rest, by being content with what he gives them, by doing their work conscientiously, and by speaking well of him.

'The virtuous man will serve his spiritual masters by affectionate deeds, by affectionate words, by affectionate thoughts, by welcoming them cordially, by providing for their material needs.

'In five ways also the spiritual masters will respond to the conduct of their disciple. They will preserve him from vice, they will encourage him to virtue, they will be full of goodwill and affection towards him, they will instruct him in spiritual truths, they will elucidate his doubts, and they will point out the way that leads to the higher worlds.

'He will be praised who is wise and lives virtuously, peaceful, prudent, and modest, always ready to give instruction. He will be praised who is energetic and vigilant, unshakable in adversity, persevering and wise. He will be honoured who is kindly, amiable, grateful, generous, who serves as a guide, as a teacher, as a leader of men.

'Generosity, courtesy, kindliness practised in all circumstances and towards one and all, are to the world what the axle is to the cart.

'Because they cherish and propagate these virtues, the Sages are worthy of praise.'

After the Enlightened One had spoken thus, Sijâla cried:

'Thy words are wonderful, O Master. It is as though one lifted up that which has been overthrown, as though one discovered that which had been hidden, as though one led back to the straight road the traveller who had lost his way, as though one lit a lamp in the darkness so that those who had eyes could see what was around them. Thus, the Venerable One, by many comparisons, has made me know the truth.

'I put my faith in thee, Lord, in the Law and in the Community; receive me as thy disciple from today to the end of my life.'

# THE MAHAMANGALA SUTTA

## DISCOURSE ON THE BEATITUDES

THUS have I heard. The Exalted One was once sojourning hard by Savatthi in Jeta's grove in the monastery of Anatha Pindika. Now one night a certain *Deva*, illumining the whole Jetavana with his radiance, came where the Exalted One was, and bowed down in salutation to him, and stood on one side. And so standing, the *Deva* addressed the Exalted One in the following stanza:

1. Many *Devas* and men
   Have held various things to be blessings
   When they were longing for happiness;
   Do thou declare unto us the highest good.

The Exalted One answers:

2. Not to serve the foolish,
   But to serve the wise,
   To honour those worthy of honour,
      This is the greatest blessing.

3. To dwell in a pleasant land,
   To have done good works in a former birth,
   To cherish right desires in the heart,
      This is the greatest blessing.

4. Much clarity and much learning,
    And mastery over one's self,
    And a pleasant manner of speech,
      This is the greatest blessing.

5. To support father and mother,
    To cherish wife and child,
    To follow a peaceful calling,
      This is the greatest blessing.

6. To give alms and to live uprightly,
    To give help to one's kindred;
    And to act, without reproach,
      These are the greatest blessings.

7. To abhor and cease from sin,
    To abstain from strong drink,
    To weary not in well-doing,
      These are the greatest blessings.

8. Reverence and lowliness,
    Contentment and gratitude,
    The hearing of the Doctrine at due seasons,
      These are the greatest blessings.

9. To be patient and gentle,
    To foregather with lovers of peace,
    To speak in reason of spiritual things,
      These are the greatest blessings.

10. Self-restraint and purity,
     The knowledge of the Noble Truths,
     The realization of Nirvâna
        These are the greatest blessings.

11. The mind that is not shaken
     Amid all the leaps of life,
     That yields not to grief or passion,
        This is the greatest blessing.

12. They are scatheless on every side,
     Who set their feet in these ways;
     Their steps are attended by safety,
        And theirs is the greatest blessing.

# THE VASALA SUTTA[1]

THUS have I heard. Once upon a time the Exalted One was sojourning hard by Savatthi, in Jetavana, in the monastery of Anatha Pindika. There the Exalted One having put on his raiment in the morning, and having taken his bowl and his robes, entered Savatthi in quest of alms.

Now, at that time in the house of the Brahmana Aggika Bharadvaja the sacrificial fire was blazing and the offering was brought forth. Then the Exalted One, begging from house to house, came to the house of Brahmana Aggika Bharadvaja. The Brahmana Aggika Bharadvaja saw the Exalted One coming at a distance, and seeing him he exclaimed thus: 'Stop there, O Shaveling; stop there, O wretched Sramana; stop there, O outcast!' When this was said, the Exalted One replied thus to Brahmana Aggika Bharadvaja, 'Dost thou know, O Brahmana, what is an outcast or the things that make an outcast? Hearken, O Brahmana, and I will tell thee.' And the Exalted One spake thus:

'The man who is angry and bears hatred, who is malicious and a hypocrite, who professes false views, and is deceitful, let him be known as an outcast.

[1] This Sutta belongs to the Hinâyânist Scriptures.

'Whosoever in this world harms living beings, whether once or twice born, and in whom there is no compassion for living things, let him be known as an outcast.

'Whosoever destroys or lays siege to villages and towns, and is known as an enemy, let him be known as an outcast.

'Whether in the village or in the forest, whosoever appropriates by theft what is the property of others, and what has not been given, let him be known as an outcast.

'Whosoever having truly contracted a debt, drives away his creditor, saying: "There is no debt owing to thee," let him be known as an outcast.

'Whosoever for love of a trifle attacks a wayfarer and takes the trifle, let him be known as an outcast.

'The man who for his own sake, or for that of others, or for the sake of wealth, speaks falsely when called as a witness, let him be known as an outcast.

'Whosoever has unlawful relations with the wives of members of his family or of his friends, whether by force or with their consent, let him be known as an outcast.

'Whosoever being able does not support mother or father, when old and past their youth, let him be known as an outcast.

'Whosoever wounds by words or by blows his mother, father, brother, sister, uncle, or aunt, let him be known as an outcast.

'Whosoever when questioned as to what is good gives evil counsel, and devises evil in secret, let him be known as an outcast.

'Whosoever having committed a sin hopes: "May no one know that I have done it," and who does wrong in secret, let him be known as an outcast.

'Whosoever having gone to another's house and partaken of his good cheer does not return his hospitality when that other comes to his house, let him be known as an outcast.

'Whosoever by falsehood deceives either a Brahmana or a Sramana or any other mendicant, let him be known as an outcast.

'Whosoever by words annoys either a Brahmana or Sramana who has come at a meal-time, and does not give him anything, let him be known as an outcast.

'Whosoever is wrapt in ignorance, and gives not even a trifle, but speaks ill of (such gifts), let him be known as an outcast.

'Whosoever exalts himself and despises others through pride, being himself mean, let him be known as an outcast.

'He who excites anger in others, is avaricious, has base desires, is envious and cunning, and is not ashamed or afraid of sin, let him be known as an outcast.

'Whosoever reviles the Buddha or his disciples, a wandering mendicant or a householder, let him be known as an outcast.

'Whosoever is no saint (arhat) and yet pretends to be a saint, he is the greatest thief in all the worlds, including that of the Brahmas; he is indeed the lowest outcast.

'These whom I have described to you are indeed called outcasts.

'Not by birth does one become an outcast; not by birth does one become a Brahmana; by deeds one becomes an outcast; by deeds one become a Brahmana.

# EXTRACTS FROM THE DHAMMAPADA[1]

'VIGILANCE is the way of immortality (the Deathless). Heedlessness is the way of death. Those that are vigilant do not die. Those that are heedless are already as though dead.

'Those who know these things, those who know how to meditate, they take this delight in meditation, and in the knowledge of the Noble.

'By meditation and perseverance, by tireless energy, the wise attain to Nirvâna, the supreme beatitude.

'He who meditates earnestly, he who is pure in conduct and mindful of every action, he who is self-restrained and righteous in his life, the fame of such a one shall increase.

'By diligent attention, by reflection, by temperance, by self-mastery, the man of understanding makes for himself an island that no flood can overwhelm.

'Do not give yourselves over to heedlessness. Have naught to do with the lusts of the flesh. The vigilant man, who is given to meditation, he will attain to abundant happiness.

'When the wise man in his vigilance puts away heedlessness and ascends the tower of wisdom, he looks down,

[1] A celebrated collection of sayings attributed to the Buddha.

being free from sorrow, upon the sorrow-laden race of mankind. As from a mountain-top, the wise man looks down upon the foolish men in the valley.

'Vigilant among the heedless, waking among those who slumber, as a fleet courser outstrips a sorry nag, so the wise go their way.

'By yourselves must the effort be made; the Tathâgatas do but make known the way.

'Conquer wrath with benevolence, overcome evil with good. Confound the niggardly with liberality, and with truth the speaker of falsehoods.

'Even as a solid rock is unshaken by the wind, so are the wise unmoved by praise or by blame.

'Whoso seeks his own welfare by devising injury to another, he is entangled in hatred, and does not attain to freedom.

'Let your words be truth, and give not way to anger; give of your little to him that asks of you; by these three things men go to the realm of the gods.

'He who refrains from action when it is the time to act, he who, in his youth and strength, gives himself over to idleness, he whose will and whose spirit are feeble, this slothful man shall never find the way that leads to Wisdom.

'Stem the torrent with all thy might, O Brahmana. Having understood how the formations (samskaras) are dissolved, thou wilt understand that which is not formed (which is not a group of impermanent elements).

'It is not plaited hair, nor birth, nor wealth that makes

the Brahmana. He in whom truth and justice reside, he is happy, he is a Brahmana.[1]

'Of what avail thy plaited hair, O witless one? Of what avail thy goatskin garment? Within there is disorder: thou carest only for the outer man.

'I do not call him "a Brahmana" who is born of such a family or such a mother. He may be arrogant, he may be rich. He who is poor and detached from all things—him I call a Brahmana.

'He who has shattered all bonds,[2] he who is inaccessible to fear, he who is free from all servitude and cannot be shaken—him I call a Brahmana.

'He who has broken the thong, the cord, and the girth, he who has destroyed all obstacles, he who is the Awakened—him I call a Brahmana.

'He from whom the delights of the senses fall away as water from the petal of the lotus or a mustard seed from the point of a needle—him do I call Brahmana.

'He who in this world has been able to set a term to his suffering, he who has set down his burden, he whom nothing can trouble, him do I call a Brahmana.

'He whose knowledge is profound, he who possesses wisdom, who discerns the right path from the wrong, who has attained the highest aim, him do I call a Brahmana.

'He who holds himself apart, both from laymen and from monks, who contents himself with little and does

---

[1] Here Brahmana signifies one who has attained to spiritual illumination.
[2] The *Asavas*: sensuality, belief in a permanent *ego*, illusion and ignorance.

not beat upon other men's doors—him do I call a Brahmana.

'He who uses no violence, whether to the weak or the strong, who neither slays nor causes to be slain—him do I call a Brahmana.

'He who is tolerant with the intolerant, gentle with the violent, without greed among the grasping—him do I call a Brahmana.

'He from whom envy, hatred, pride and hypocrisy have fallen away like a mustard-seed placed on the point of a needle—him do I call a Brahmana.

'He whose speech is instructive and truthful and without harshness, offending none—him do I call a Brahmana.

'He who no longer covets aught, whether in this world or another, he who is unattached and inaccessible to trouble—him do I call a Brahmana.

'He who is free from all ties, whom knowledge preserves from questioning, who has attained to the depths where death is not—him do I call a Brahmana.

'He who in this world has shaken off the two chains; the chain of Good and the chain of Evil; who is pure and exempt from suffering and passion—him do I call a Brahmana.

'He who in his serenity, his purity, his changeless peace is radiant as the flawless moon, who has dried up within him the source of all joy—him do I call a Brahmana.

'He who has traversed the miry path, the inextricable world, so difficult to traverse, and all its vanities, he also, having achieved the passage, and has reached the further shore, who is meditative, unshaken, exempt from doubts, unattached and satisfied—him do I call a Brahmana.

'He who, putting off all human ties, has risen above all divine ties, who has liberated himself from every tie —him do I call a Brahmana.

'He who has rejected that which causes pleasure and that which causes suffering, he who is impassive, liberated from all germs,[1] the hero who has raised himself above all the worlds—him do I call a Brahmana.'

[1] The *upadhis*—which comprise the five constituents of the group called a 'person': form, sensations, perception, mental activity, consciousness, desire, error, and attachment to works.

# THE SECT OF MEDITATION

LACK of space in the present volume has prevented me from undertaking the study of the doctrines and methods peculiar to the Buddhist Mahâyânist sect known as the Sect of Meditation (*T'san* in Chinese, *Zen* in Japanese). It would take a separate volume to explain to Western readers the curious and extremely interesting interpretation which the doctors of this sect have given to Buddhism. I propose to write such a volume; meanwhile I must limit myself to indicating briefly the general tendencies of this school, which is still flourishing today among the intellectual élite of Japan.[1]

The following passage is taken from a booklet by S. Ogata, a Japanese monk. It should be noted that the term *zen*, which means 'meditation', has become in ordinary usage the name of the doctrine professed by the disciples of Bodhidharma, an Indian Buddhist philosopher who went to China about the year 520.

'What is Zen?—Zen is not simply a religion or a philosophy, but something more: it is Life itself.

'Zen is a special transmission (of conceptions and methods) outside the canonical Scriptures; which does not depend on any text.'

[1] On this subject, see the works in the English language of Professor T. D. Suzuki.

As Bodhidharma declared, Zen does not concern itself with the discussion of abstruse notions such as God or Truth; what Zen demands of the disciple is that he should 'behold his own face.'

We may say that the whole doctrine of Zen is contained in the famous injunction of the sixth Patriarch of the sect: Weï-Lang 638–713):

'Think not of good, think not of evil, but consider thine own countenance as it is at this moment, the countenance which was thine even before thou wast born.'

'The most important point in the teaching of the sect of Meditation is introspection,' says Mr. Dih Ping Tsze, a contemporary Chinese adherent of the sect. 'Introspection or introversion means the turning of one's own "light" to shine inwardly. . . . The disciples of Zen direct their attention inwards and reflect exclusively upon their own "real nature", known in Chinese as the "natural countenance." '

The Patriarch Weï-Lang describes meditation (Dhyana) and 'concentration' (samadhi) as follows:

'Dhyana means to be free from attachment to all outer objects and samadhi means to attain inner peace. . . . When our mind works freely without any hindrance and is at liberty to come or to go, then we attain to the concentration (samadhi) of wisdom (prajñâ), but to refrain from thinking of anything, so that all thoughts are suppressed, is to be Dharma-ridden, and this is false and pernicious.'

In one of his sermons Weï-Lang said:

'. . . When the fifth Patriarch preached to me, I became enlightened so soon as he had spoken, and spontaneously I realized the true nature of *Tâthâta* (Suchness, Identity). For this reason, it is my particular object to propagate the teaching of the 'Sudden School', so that the learners may become enlightened immediately, and realize their true nature by introspection.

'Should they fail to enlighten themselves, they ought to ask the learned Buddhists who understand the teaching of the Mâhâyana to show them the right way. On the other hand, those who enlighten themselves need no extraneous help. It is wrong to insist upon the notion that without the advice of the learned we cannot obtain liberation. Why?—Because it is by our innate wisdom that we enlighten ourselves, and even the extraneous help and instructions of a learned friend would be unavailing if we were deluded by false doctrines and erroneous views.'

Zen is in complete agreement with the Tibetan Mahâyânist sects which affirm the basic identity of *Nirvâna* and *samsâra*. This is why its spiritual masters tell their disciples not to seek for 'illumination' outside the world.[1]

Again, Weï-Lang says:

'The kingdom of Buddhism is in the world, within which we must seek enlightenment. To seek enlightenment by separating oneself from this world is as absurd as to search for rabbit's horns.'

'Right views are called transcendent; erroneous views are called worldly. When views, whether right or erroneous, are discarded, then the essence of knowledge (enlightenment) manifests itself.' (Sutra of Weï-Lang.)

In one of his sermons the Master Ta-hui indicates in a striking fashion the aim of the Buddhist's spiritual training:

'Whence comes birth? Whither goes death? He who knows this "Whence" and "Whither" is said to be a true Buddhist. But who is this that knows birth and death? Who is this that suffers births and deaths? Who is this that does not know whence birth comes and whither death goes? Who is this that suddenly comes to the realization of this "Whence" and "Whither"? When these things are not thoroughly understood, the eyes wander, the heart beats fast, the bowels are writhen, as though a ball of fire were rolling up and down inside the body. And who is it that undergoes this torture? If you would know who he is, dive down into the depths of your being, which no intellection can possibly reach; and when you know it, you know also that there is a place which neither birth nor death can touch.'

# MISCELLANEOUS

'TELL him, I look for no recompense—not even to be reborn in heaven—but I seek the welfare of men, to bring back those that have gone astray, to enlighten those that live in the night of error, to banish from the world all pain and all suffering.' (*Fo-sho-hing-tsan-ching.*)

'Which, O disciples, think you is greater; the tears which you have poured out, wailing and lamenting, during this long pilgrimage, ever hastening toward new births and new deaths; joined to the unloved, separated from the loved—these, or the waters of the great ocean? Without beginning and without end is this *samsara*. Unknowable is the beginning of beings wrapped in ignorance, who through desire are led to ever-renewed birth, and so pursue the round of rebirth. Thus for long have you suffered sorrow and pain and misfortune and fed the graveyards full; long enough truly to become dissatisfied with all existence; long enough to turn away from all existence; long enough to break loose from it all.' (*Samyutta Nikâya.*)

'Be steadfast in the performance of duties great and small. Lead a life free from blame and in accordance with the precepts, and let your speech be of like nature.' (*Mahaparanibbâna Sutta.*)

'There is no happiness apart from righteousness.' (*Attanagaluvimsa*.)

'What is a real gift? A gift for which no sort of return is expected.' (*Prasnottaramalika*.)

'Even if a man has power over others, yet ought he to be gentle with the weak.' (*Udanavarga*.)

'Like food besmeared with poison, I abhor such happiness as is tainted with unrighteousness.' (*Jatakamala*.)

'The distinctive signs of true religions are good-will, love, truthfulness, purity, nobility of feeling and kindness.' (*Asoka Inscription*.)

'The layman who follows the doctrines will not be addicted to strong drink. He will never invite anyone to drink, neither will he approve of drinking in another, since he knows that the end of intemperance is madness. Through the habit of drunkenness, fools fall into sin, and induce others to drink. Men should shun this haunt of all ills, this delirium, this folly in which only the witless find their joy.' (*Dhammika Sutta*.)

'If you speak to a woman, do so in purity of heart. Say to yourself: "Placed in this sinful world, let me be as the spotless lily, that takes no taint from the mire in which it grows." Is she old: regard her as your mother. Is she of high degree: look upon her as your sister. Is she of lowly birth: think of her as a younger sister. Is she a child: treat her with deference and politeness.' (*Sûtra in 42 Sections*.)

'Whatsoever may be the cause of your suffering, do not wound another.' (*Udanavarga*.)

'Follow the path of duty; show kindness to thy brothers and lead them not into suffering.' (*Avadana Sutta.*)

'Whoso hurts and harms living creatures, destitute of sympathy for any living thing, let him be known as an outcast.' (*Vasala Sutta.*)

'A noble truth I would discover; an aim unlike the common aims of men. I would make an end of the pain that springs from existence.' (*Fo-sho-hing-tsan-ching.*)

'Not for the sake of my own well-being do I practise universal benevolence; but I love benevolence, because it is my desire to contribute to the happiness of living beings.' (*Jatakamala.*)

'The truly virtuous will help those in need out of pure compassionateness, and not from any hope of personal gain, caring little whether their good deed is seen of another or not.' (*Jatakamala.*)

'The disciple lives as a reconciler of those who are divided, as one who binds still more closely those who are friends; as an establisher of peace, a preparer of peace; uttering always the words of peace.' (*Tevijja Sutta.*)

'Not superstitious rites, but kindness to servants and inferiors, respect for those who deserve respect, self-control, wedded to kindness in dealing with living creatures, these and virtuous deeds of like nature are verily the rites that ought everywhere to be performed.' (*Asoka Inscription.*)

'Good-will toward all beings is the true religion.' (*Buddhacarita.*)

'Cherish in your hearts boundless good-will to all that lives.' (*Metta Sutta.*)

'Whoso is condemned by the world, let him not cherish feelings of enmity against it.' (*Sammaparibbajaniya Sutta.*)

'Whoso, when he is reviled, lets not resentment find a place in his heart, has won a shining victory.' (*Udanavarga.*)

'Carrying neither staff nor sword, sympathetic and kindly, the disciple bears love and compassion toward all living creatures.' (*Majjhima Nikâya.*)

'If you wish to show your respect for the departed Buddha, follow the example he has set you of patience and forbearance.' (*Fo-sho-hing-tsan-ching.*)

'As the high rocky mountain-range stands unmoved amidst the storm, so do the truly wise stand unshaken, alike in praise and in blame.' (*Dhammapada.*)

'All beings long for happiness; therefore extend thy compassion to all., (*Mahavamsa.*)

'Trust in outward help brings distress; only trust in one's self brings strength and joy.' (*Fo-sho-hing-tsan-ching.*)

'True worship does not consist in the offering of incense, flowers, and other material things, but in striving ever toward the same goal as him whom we adore.' (*Jatakamala.*)

'To give food to a simple honest man (in need) is infinitely greater in point of merit than to devote oneself to the study of questions relating to heaven and earth, spirits and demons, such as occupy so many.' (*Sûtra of the 42 Sections.*)

'Wherein does religion consist? It consists in doing as little harm as possible, in doing good in abundance, in the practice of love, of compassion, of truthfulness and purity, in all the walks of life.' (*Asoka Inscription*.)

'The real treasure is that which consists of charity and pity, temperance and self-control. This hidden treasure is secure and does not perish. Though he leave the fleeting riches of the world, this man carries with him a treasure whose possession does no wrong to others, and which no thief can steal.' (*Nidhikanda Sutta*.)

'Do not decry other sects, do not depreciate others, but rather honour whatever in them is worthy of honour.' (*Asoka Inscription*.)

'Even if those who are not of us, O disciples, should give utterance to harsh words concerning me, or my doctrine, or my companions, yet is this no reason why you should give way to anger.' (*Brahmajala Sutta*.)

'What does it matter to thee whether another be guilty or guiltless? Come, friend, and look to thine own ways.' (*Amagandha Sutta*.)

'Note this well, Gotami: a doctrine, whatever its origin, if it leads to passion and not to peace, to pride and not to modesty, to greater desire and not to moderation, to the love of society and not to the love of solitude, to idleness and not to earnest striving, to a violent spirit and not to peaceable spirit—that doctrine is not the Doctrine; it is not the Discipline; it is not the teaching of the Master.' (*Vinâya Pitaka*.)

'After you have studied the Doctrine, let your purified

hearts find their delight in bringing forth corresponding deeds.' (*Fo-sho-hing-tsan-ching*.)

'Better it is for me to die in battle with the tempter than to be vanquished by him and yet continue to live.' (*Padhama Sutta*.)

'A courteous behaviour keeps the heart at peace; that lacking, the seed of every virtue dies.' (*Fo-sho-hing-tsan-ching*.)

'Courtesy is the most precious of jewels. Beauty without courtesy is like a garden without flowers.' (*Buddhacarita*.)

'Half-hearted attention prepares the way for new errors and delusions, and allows old errors to increase. Sustained attention does not allow new errors to arise, and destroys the old.' (*Majjhima Nikaya*.)

'Above all things be not heedless. Heedlessness is the foe of all the virtues.' (*Fo-sho-hing-tsan-ching*.)

'I adjure you, O disciples, for your own sakes be diligent. Devote yourselves to the purification of your own minds. Be earnest, be persevering, be attentive, be thoughtful, for your own salvation.' (*Mahâparinibbana Sutta*.)

'The true disciple has put away sloth and idleness; he is free from heedless lassitude. Loving the light, intelligent and perspicacious, he purifies his heart from all heedlessness and sloth.' (*Majjhima Sutta*.)

'Even though the body is clothed in the layman's habit, yet may the spirit rise to the highest things. The man of the world and the hermit differ not from each other if both alike have conquered selfishness. So long as the heart is bound by the fetters of sensuality, all outward tokens of the ascetics are vain.' (*Fo-sho-hing-tsan-ching*.)

'Even though robbers and murderers should sever your limbs and joints with a saw, if you therefore gave way to anger you would not be following my teaching. Thus rather, my disciples, ought you to behave: Your spirit should not be moved, no evil word should escape your lips; you should remain benevolent, with your heart full of love and void of secret malice; and you should enfold these men (the malefactors) with loving thoughts, with thoughts, generous, deep, and limitless, purged of all anger and hate. Even thus, my disciples, ought ye to do.' (*Majjhima Nikâya*.)

'Subdue rage. Do not yield to the impulse of a turbulent heart. He who can calm his heart when it suddenly burns with angry passion, he truly may be called a skilful charioteer.' (*Fo-sho-hing-tsan-ching*.)

'To make an end of self-seeking, that is blessedness.' (*Udanavarga*.)

'When he who does good ceases to concern himself with the result of his action, ambition and anger disappear.' (*Lalita Vistara*.)

'Strive with all your strength, and let not sloth find a place in your hearts.' (*Fo-sho-hing-tsan-ching*.)

'The wise man does not stand still; he goes forward always toward a brighter light.' (*Fo-sho-hing-tsan-ching*.)

'What is the root of evil? Envy, hatred, illusion, are the roots of evil. And what are the roots of good? To be free from envy, hatred, and illusion are the roots of good.' (*Majjhima Nikâya*.)

'The notion "I myself" enters only into the thoughts of the foolish. The wise man knows that there is no foundation for such a belief. Searching the world with true vision, he comes to the conclusion that all is void, and subject to swift decay. One thing alone endures unbroken: the Law. When a man has attained to this insight, then he sees the truth.' (*Fo-sho-hing-tsan-ching*.)

'Strictly speaking, the duration of the life of a living being does not exceed the duration of a thought. Just as a chariot, as it moves, rolls only on one point of the tire, and when it is resting rests only on one point, in just the same way the life of a living being lasts only for the period of a single thought. As soon as that thought has ceased, the being may be regarded as having ceased.'[1] (*Visuddhi Magga*.)

'Hell was not created by anyone. The fire of an angry mind produces the fire of hell and consumes its possessor. When any person does evil he lights the fire of hell and burns in his own fire.' (*Mulamuli*.)

'Entangled in the meshes of speculation, the inexperienced son of earth never wins free from the bondage of old age and death, sorrow and pain, grief and despair; he never wins free, I say, from sorrow.' (*Majjhima Nikâya*.)

'Whoso has understood this world to its foundations

---

[1] Because when this thought came the 'group' which constitutes the momentary personality is no longer what it was the moment before.

and perceived the highest truth; whoso has crossed the ever-flowing stream of existence, and, free from all fetters, has subdued passion, such a one is called wise by those of understanding.' (*Muni Sutta.*)

'With the comprehension of the impermanent and intrinsically moral nature of all things, which are subject to suffering, arises the sun of true wisdom; wanting this comprehension there can be no true enlightenment. In this comprehension alone lies the goal. Whoso seeks not to attain it will be torn to pieces by death.' (*Fo-sho-hing-tsan-ching.*)

'Wander through the land converting those that are still unconverted, acting as teachers to this pain-riven world, and wheresoever the darkness of ignorance reigns, there kindle the light. Thus go ye forth, filled with compassion, bringing salvation to all.' (*Fo-sho-hing-tsan-ching.*)

# INDEX

# DISCUS BOOKS

### DISTINGUISHED NON-FICTION

## THEATER, FILM AND TELEVISION

| | | |
|---|---|---|
| **ACTORS TALK ABOUT ACTING** | | |
| Lewis Funke and John Booth, Eds. | 15062 | 1.95 |
| **ACTION FOR CHILDREN'S TELEVISION** | 10090 | 1.25 |
| **ANTONIN ARTAUD**  Bettina L. Knapp | 12062 | 1.65 |
| **A BOOK ON THE OPEN THEATER**  Robert Pasoli | 12047 | 1.65 |
| **THE CONCISE ENCYCLOPEDIC GUIDE TO SHAKESPEARE** | | |
| Michael Martin and Richard Harrier, Eds. | 16832 | 2.65 |
| **THE DISNEY VERSION**  Richard Schnickel | 08953 | 1.25 |
| **EDWARD ALBEE: A PLAYWRIGHT IN PROTEST** | | |
| Michael E. Rutenberg | 11916 | 1.65 |
| **THE EMPTY SPACE**  Peter Brook | 32763 | 1.95 |
| **EXPERIMENTAL THEATER**  James Roose-Evans | 11981 | 1.65 |
| **FOUR CENTURIES OF SHAKESPEARIAN CRITICISM** | | |
| Frank Kermode, Ed. | 20131 | 1.95 |
| **GUERILLA STREET THEATRE**  Henry Lesnick, Ed. | 15198 | 2.45 |
| **THE HOLLYWOOD SCREENWRITERS** | | |
| Richard Corliss | 12450 | 1.95 |
| **IN SEARCH OF LIGHT: THE BROADCASTS OF** | | |
| **EDWARD R. MURROW**  Edward Bliss, Ed. | 19372 | 1.95 |
| **INTERVIEWS WITH FILM DIRECTORS** | | |
| Andrew Sarris | 21568 | 1.95 |
| **MOVIES FOR KIDS**  Edith Zornow and Ruth Goldstein | 17012 | 1.65 |
| **PICTURE**  Lillian Ross | 08839 | 1.25 |
| **THE LIVING THEATRE**  Pierre Biner | 17640 | 1.65 |
| **PUBLIC DOMAIN**  Richard Schechner | 12104 | 1.65 |
| **RADICAL THEATRE NOTEBOOK**  Arthur Sainer | 22442 | 2.65 |
| **SOMETHING WONDERFUL RIGHT AWAY** | | |
| Jeffrey Sweet | 37119 | 2.95 |

## GENERAL NON-FICTION

| | | |
|---|---|---|
| **ADDING A DIMENSION**  Isaac Asimov | 36871 | 1.50 |
| **A TESTAMENT**  Frank Lloyd Wright | 12039 | 1.65 |
| **AMBIGUOUS AFRICA**  Georges Balandier | 25288 | 2.25 |
| **THE AMERICAN CHALLENGE** | | |
| J. J. Servan Schreiber | 11965 | 1.65 |
| **AMERICA THE RAPED**  Gene Marine | 09373 | 1.25 |
| **ARE YOU RUNNING WITH ME, JESUS?** | | |
| Malcolm Boyd | 09993 | 1.25 |
| **THE AWAKENING OF INTELLIGENCE**  J. Krishnamurti | 45674 | 3.50 |
| **THE BIOGRAPHY OF ALICE B. TOKLAS**  Linda Simon | 39073 | 2.95 |
| **THE BOOK OF IMAGINARY BEINGS** | | |
| Jorge Luis Borges | 11080 | 1.45 |
| **BUILDING THE EARTH**  Pierre de Chardin | 08938 | 1.25 |
| **CHEYENNE AUTUMN**  Mari Sandoz | 39255 | 2.25 |
| **THE CHILD IN THE FAMILY**  Maria Montessori | 28118 | 1.50 |
| **THE CHILDREN'S REPUBLIC**  Edward Mobius | 21337 | 1.50 |
| **CHINA: SCIENCE WALKS ON TWO LEGS** | | |
| Science for the People | 20123 | 1.75 |
| **CLASSICS REVISITED**  Kenneth Rexroth | 08920 | 1.25 |

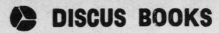

# DISCUS BOOKS

## DISTINGUISHED NON-FICTION

| | | |
|---|---|---|
| THE CONCISE ENCYCLOPEDIC GUIDE TO SHAKESPEARE   Michael Rheta Martin and Richard A. Harrier | 16832 | 2.65 |
| CONSCIOUSNESS AND REALITY Charles Museous and Arthur M. Young, Eds. | 18903 | 2.45 |
| CONVERSATIONS WITH JORGE LUIS BORGES Richard Burgin | 11908 | 1.65 |
| CORTES AND MONTEZUMA   Maurice Collis | 40402 | 2.50 |
| DISINHERITED   Dave Van Every | 09555 | 1.25 |
| DIVISION STREET: AMERICA   Studs Terkel | 22780 | 2.25 |
| EINSTEIN: THE LIFE AND TIMES   Ronald W. Clark | 44123 | 3.95 |
| ESCAPE FROM FREEDOM   Erich Fromm | 47472 | 2.95 |
| THE FEMALE IMAGINATION   Patricia Meyer Spacks | 28142 | 2.45 |
| THE FEMINIZATION OF AMERICAN CULTURE Ann Douglas | 38513 | 2.95 |
| FRONTIERS OF CONSCIOUSNESS John White, ed. | 24810 | 2.50 |
| GAY AMERICAN HISTORY   Jonathan Katz, Ed. | 40550 | 3.95 |
| GERMANS   George Bailey | 20644 | 1.95 |
| GERTRUDE STEIN: A COMPOSITE PORTRAIT Linda Simon, Ed. | 20115 | 1.65 |
| THE GREAT POLITICAL THEORIES, VOL. I Michael Curtis | 23119 | 1.95 |
| THE GREAT POLITICAL THEORIES, VOL. II Michael Curtis | 23127 | 1.95 |
| THE GREEK WAY   Edith Hamilton | 37481 | 2.25 |
| GROTOWSKI   Raymond Temkine | 12278 | 1.65 |
| THE HEBREW GODDESS   Raphael Patai | 39289 | 2.95 |
| HENRY JAMES: Five Volume Biography   Leon Edel | 39636 | 14.75 |
| HOMOSEXUAL: LIBERATION AND OPPRESSION Dennis Altman | 14214 | 1.65 |
| THE HUMAN USE OF HUMAN BEINGS Norbert Wiener | 21584 | 1.95 |
| THE INCAS   Garcilaso de la Vega | 11999 | 1.65 |
| INTERPRETATION OF DREAMS   Freud | 38828 | 2.95 |
| JESUS IN BAD COMPANY   Adolf Holl | 19281 | 1.65 |
| THE LIFE AND DEATH OF LENIN   Robert Payne | 12161 | 1.65 |
| THE LIFE AND WORK OF WILHELM REICH M. Cattier | 14928 | 1.65 |
| LIFE IN A CRYSTAL PALACE   Alan Harrington | 15784 | 1.65 |
| THE LIFE OF JOHN MAYNARD KEYNES R. F. Harrod | 12625 | 2.45 |
| LOUISA MAY: A MODERN BIOGRAPHY Martha Saxton | 40881 | 2.95 |
| MALE AND FEMALE UNDER 18 Nancy Larrick and Eve Merriam, Eds. | 29645 | 1.50 |
| POE, POE, POE . . .   Daniel Hoffman | 41459 | 2.95 |
| MAN IN THE TRAP   Elsworth F. Baker. Ph.D. | 18809 | 1.95 |
| MAWSON'S WILL   Lennard Bickel | 39131 | 2.50 |

(2) DDB 9-79

# DISCUS BOOKS
## DISTINGUISHED NON-FICTION

*The Everest of consciousness*

Madame Alexandra David-Neel, a daring Parisian woman who traveled throughout Tibet disguised as a beggar and became the first Westerner to penetrate the sacred city of Lhasa in over 200 years, wrote this book to illuminate the deepest mysteries of Buddhism to the Western mind. It begins with a brief life of the Buddha, Prince Siddhartha Guatama, then moves into discussions of the theory of Interdependent Origins, the Buddhist science of reality as an eternally flickering cinema of cause and effect; The Eightfold Path, the way to attain Buddhahood; the concept of Karma, the fate within; and Nirvana, the door to infinity, the reality beyond this dream.

Buddhism is a highly personal religious philosophy, manifested in myriad ways. This book provides lucid explanations of the general dynamics of Buddhism with special insights into the Tantric-Mahayanist tradition of Tibet, as well as excerpts from original sutras and a short consideration of the sect of meditation, Zen.

"This is a fresh, straightforward introduction to Buddhist philosophy. ... A true scholar, David-Neel distinguishes between legend, opinion and essential Buddhist theory. A lively and unconventional teacher, she employs amusing anecdotes from her travels in the East to entertain and educate the Western reader."     *Los Angeles Times*

*WITH A FOREWORD BY CHRISTMAS HUMPHREYS*

A DISCUS BOOK/PUBLISHED BY AVON BOOKS

Printed in U.S.A.